To Jennifer James

I hope you enjoy

Peg Blackstone

Things They Never Told Me In Therapy School

Serious Problems - Surprising Solutions

Peg Blackstone, M.A.

Port Gamble Press
Kingston, Washington

Inquiries and Orders:
(206) 775-1377

Port Gamble Press,
P.O. Box 406,
Kingston, Washington 98346
USA

ISBN 0-9630291-0-X

Library of Congress Catalog Card Number: 91-66149

First Printing, September, 1991

Printed in the United States of America

Contents

Introduction

What's the deal with these psychotherapists, anyway? Haven't you ever wondered why people who write about therapy make it sound so unrelentingly heavy? And don't you hate it when authors insist on using big, important-sounding words that make personal change (and reading their books) seem so complicated and difficult? Does therapy really have to be so hard? Good questions!

I've been therapizing people since 1974, and have found the experience to be very different from the serious, intensely difficult work I expected. So have my clients. How? Well for one thing, it can be a lot of fun. Grappling with life's demands naturally entails many uncomfortable and tough sessions all right, but that's only part of the story. Hilarity, goofiness, and human sweetness punctuate many a therapeutic hour too. Just like life.

For another, folks in therapy have gotten a bad reputation. No fair! You've probably noticed how clients have been portrayed as fragile victims who need to be handled with therapeutic kid gloves. How about giving them some credit? The humans I work with are tough, smart, resourceful, and competent, and they deserve to be treated with more respect than that.

"Adult Survivors" of any kind of childhood trauma have already done the hard part long before they walk into any shrink's office. That's why they're called survivors. They met their early challenges without benefit of therapy and usually without much help from

1

anyone else. So they obviously don't need my assistance to function in the world. What I may be able to help them with is functioning more happily and easily.

From Freud on down, all the focus seems to have been on what's wrong with people. His patients were "neurotic." Nowadays people are "victims" of an "addiction" or a "disease" who must spend lots of time and money on "getting healthy." And even after all that they must remain eternally vigilant lest they backslide into "dysfunctional behavior." That all seems pretty silly to me.

What about what's Right with people? What about human guts and stubbornness? What about how clever people are and how they make perfect sense in the ways they cope with life's slings and arrows? And above all, what about how they manage to reach adulthood without going crazy or killing themselves, and then have the gumption to laugh in the face of their childhood goblins and monsters?

The folks in my waiting room aren't "neurotic", they're heroes and heroines who have a few changes they want to make in their lives. Like maybe taking off some of their armor or seeing whether they still need all those lances and shields. Stuff like that. Perhaps even deciding that there's not much call for heroes these days and opting for a career change. (Even knights of old needed a little help getting out of their armor...)

So that's what this book is about - lots of heroes and heroines and one awestruck therapist. And how we manage to make changes together while making sense. How therapy is not some complicated, ponderous process, but a journey undertaken by two adventuresome souls who have very little idea of what they are really getting into. But who nevertheless commit themselves, for better or worse, to sticking with it until they get where they were going.

If you like reading exciting and funny adventure stories about wonderful people, you'll like this book. You won't find a lot of villains in these pages, though, so don't bother looking. You will meet a lot of engaging and scrappy kids of all ages - a sort of "our gang" of psychotherapy. And you will learn what the "child within" is really all about. Eric Berne, the founder of Transactional Analysis, developed the concept years ago, and would be pleased, no doubt, to see how popular it has become.

Therapists who have read THINGS THEY NEVER TOLD ME IN THERAPY SCHOOL have found the clinical material (techniques and such) intriguing and useful. In this regard, I'd like to thank four folks who have been particularly influential as my Therapy School Teachers. They are, in order of encounter, Martin Haykin, M.D., David (Pat) Jarvis, M.D., Robert Goulding, M.D., and Mary McClure Goulding, M.S.W. Marty, Pat, Bob and Mary, thanks for being such great mentors and mentresses. The contents of this book, of course, only reflect the opinions of the author... And all the characters within are either fictional or so disguised as to be unrecognizable.

I also want to thank my family for their unfailing efforts to get me to be "less psychological." Doug, Don, Drew, Mom and Dad, you've been good sports about this invasion of your privacy. I love you all a bunch.

And finally, thanks to my swell editors, Geri Frick, Cynthia Howe, and Judy Miller. I appreciate your generosity and graciousness in being willing to donate your valuable time even after I untied you from the chairs and put down the whips. I couldn't have done it without you. Cheers!

CHAPTER 1

In the Trenches

They leave out a lot of important stuff in Therapy School. Like what to do when you're leading group and your skirt falls down. Yup, that's right, there I was at the board writing down pearls of psychotherapeutic wisdom for someone who was doing some heavy emotional work. All of a sudden, the strap on my wrap-around skirt broke, and half of it swung gracefully down along my right leg. In mid-sob, the client stopped and said "Oh, your skirt"! I heard sharp intakes of breath from around the room.

Quickly, I searched my memory for the class in Therapy School which had covered this eventuality. Was it Statistics? Maybe Early Childhood Development? Psychodiagnostics? None of them fit. I was pretty sure, though, that undressing, even accidentally, in front of your clients was not recommended. Maybe in California, but certainly not in Seattle.

In my mind, I hastily sorted through the few Therapy School concepts which seemed like they might pertain, like "Therapist Transparency." That means how much of self the therapist reveals to the client. This experience, however, gave a whole new meaning to the term. "Hysteria" seemed close, and so did "Acute Panic Disorder," but not quite right. I even thought of "Passive Aggressive Behavior," but how could a skirt be accused of that?

What to do? I decided the only solution was to wing it. Tucking the strap back in, I thanked my mother out loud for always insisting that

I wear clean underwear, (and a slip) and went right on, noting that the sky did not fall. Right then and there, I resolved to write an expose some day revealing what the experience of therapy is really like, from both sides of the couch.

Things they don't tell you in Therapy School. Fill in the gaps. One day, out there in Therapyville, some therapist's skirt is going to fall down, and because she's read this book, she'll know just what to do. Or he, not to be sexist, but that's more complicated...

There's no getting around it, psychotherapy is a peculiar way to spend your time. They don't admit this in Therapy School, but it's true. The longer I'm in practice the more I shake my head at the paradoxes - the whole procedure. And I'm bonkers about it. I even enjoy sitting on the other side of the couch in the client chair. Usually. I have managed to spend somewhat more time on the therapist side of the couch, but not by too much. I must be a believer.

So you ask, what's so odd about therapy? Well for one thing, it's the only business I know of which requires that you get exceedingly close to someone, maybe closer than they have let anyone before, and then spend your time helping them get ready to leave the relationship. Weird, huh? Especially since issues of trust, intimacy, commitment, and loss may be just what folks have come into my office to resolve. Never mind what all this coming and going is like for me.

And for another thing, it's nosy. Really nosy. I feel free to ask my clients all sorts of personal stuff, like how are their sex lives, how much do they earn, what do they fantasize about, what have they done to other people, and what have others done to them? (All of this, of course, in intimate detail). And why did they do that, and how do they feel about it? And how the heck did they get this or that idea, and what makes them think it's true, anyhow? And then I may even feel free to make editorial comments, ranging from applause to smiles and laughter to bronx cheers and even occasionally to tears. Is that nosy, or what?

If such nosiness sounds presumptuous, that's because it is. I am awed by the amount of trust in me, in themselves, and in the therapeutic process that clients muster in order to allow this intimacy. Here I go, snooping into the dusty corners of their lives, opening closets, lifting covers, moving their treasures, emptying out wastebaskets of old trash. Am I a persistent detective, thorough housecleaner, rigid inspector, fussy auntie, amused commentator, concerned parent, amazed tourist? Each, at times. The nerve...!

So why would someone consent to this invasion - much less seek it out - much less pay for the privilege? Good question. As I often say to clients, it's not most people's favorite pastime. Hardly anyone decides to come in because they happened to be in the neighborhood, or didn't have anything else on the calendar that day.

They come out of dissatisfaction. Something is not right in their lives, ranging in severity from a vague sense of something missing to consideration of suicide. Pat Jarvis, my psychiatric consultant, (known as "Pat the Psychiatrist" to my clients and trainees) has a phrase he uses to describe everyone's job in life: "To live in this world, and be satisfied, and happy with self and others." If a person is not doing some part of this job adequately she comes into therapy to change that.

Pat presents a simple statement here, but it's profound. Take the first part, "To live in this world..." That doesn't mean a fantasy world or the past or the future or the world as you wish it were or the world as you think it ought to be but this world; as is - reality - warts and all. You'd be surprised how many folks aren't doing this. And aren't aware of it.

"...and be satisfied..." What does that boil down to? Well it may mean that the person does not know how to derive satisfaction out of everyday accomplishments or out of finishing steps in a sequence. He may say to himself, "I can't feel good until I'm the best," (Or until it was done perfectly. Or until he's reached the top.) This client might call home to announce an exciting promotion to bank vice-president and his parent might say, "Great, maybe some day you'll be president." Get the idea?

Many people never develop a positive, workable concept of "good enough." It's not the accomplishment, but what one does with it in one's head that produces satisfaction or dissatisfaction. For example, I can make an intervention with someone that I know has helped them change their entire life course, maybe even helped them to decide never to kill themselves. An exquisite therapeutic move. And I can feel excited about that or I can feel bad about it by asking myself why I didn't think of doing it six months sooner.

Or maybe the person is in a situation that is just plain icky. He can't be satisfied and happy unless he changes it. Like the client who came in and wanted me to help him stop being jealous. After he described the circumstances of his relationship I said "I can't do that. If you weren't jealous here I'd wonder why not. I can help you change your part in this dance the two of you are doing so that you start having the relationship you want and we'll see how she responds."

"Doing this may involve your being more jealous. And less `reasonable.' And less `understanding.' And nicer too, because you'll like her better if you don't let her treat you so badly." He did all of the above and is now married to the lady and living mostly happily ever after. (Totally happily ever after occurs only in fairy tales; mostly happily ever after is achievable.)

Lots of folks won't let themselves make the changes they need to because they tell themselves they should be satisfied with their situation and something must be wrong with them if they aren't. So they try and try to screw their heads around to the point where they feel the way they think they should. Where they have the proper emotions. I wish I had a nickel for every time a client has said to me, "Anyone else would feel lucky to be in my shoes; why don't I?" Well, if they go into group therapy and describe their circumstances, it turns out that "anyone else" in fact would feel about the same as they do. Maybe even be more upset.

There can be more than meets the eye to being satisfied. Sometimes you need to change what you're doing in your head, sometimes, what you're doing out there in the world. More often, both. Even biological factors need to be considered - a person can be anhedonic (good Therapy School word - it means unable to derive satisfaction) because she is depressed. So the depression needs to be understood and dealt with as a prerequisite to getting hedonic.

"...and happy with self and others." Hmmm. That's a biggie, isn't it? Eric Berne came up with the term, "I'm OK, You're OK." That's what "happy with self and others" is about. Most folks come through my door deeply believing in badness. Oh, it's not always right out in the open, but lurking underneath a sophisticated veneer may be a much younger, more primitive conviction that "There's something really wrong with me. And I'm here for Peg to find out what it is, tell me, and fix it so I'll get better."

Therapy is not a self-improvement course. People don't really start feeling happier till they begin to figure out that they aren't in my office to get better. They were fine when they came in. Problem usually is, they don't know that on a reliable level. They're still trying to earn their Place in Heaven.

"...and others." The flip side of self-badness is other-badness. Because if badness is around here anywhere it has to belong to someone. So a lot of other-blaming turns out to be a defense against self-blaming, which usually is at the bottom of it all. One name for this concept is "hot potato." No one wants to be left holding the badness, so they toss it to someone else - "it's yours, no, here, it's yours," etc.

But the deal is, you can't get satisfaction or happiness with self and others till you get rid of people-badness entirely. No Blame. No Fault. Blame is different from responsibility. Good thing, too, because therapeutic change is based on taking appropriate responsibility for one's life course. In "The Theory and Practice of Group Psychotherapy," Irvin Yalom, M.D., offers four basic therapeutic premises that illustrate this:

1. Only I can change the world I have created for myself.
2. There is no danger in change.
3. To attain what I really want, I must change.
4. I can change, I am potent. (p. 157)

Notice that what he is talking about changing is the world (view) one has created, not the human who has created it. No one is bad or perverse for having created their special frame of reference; the conclusions and beliefs underlying it always make sense. So taking responsibility for having authored one's life does not equate with taking blame for having done so. Good. Otherwise, who would accept such responsibility? You'd have to be weird.

For example, I'm responsible if I'm not very trusting of others because I grew up believing people will let me down, but that doesn't mean I'm bad for having concluded that and need to wallow in self-blame. Yet, as Stanford Education Professor Ray McDermott says, "Our language is loaded in favor of finding blame - sticking it to them." What a deal. (25, p.12)

So, many folks come for therapy willing to submit to much nosiness in order that their badnesses can be sniffed out, and hopefully snuffed out. "We have gathered here today to examine the life of Alphonse Client and expose him for what he really is so that we can improve him..." This sort of inner expectation about what therapy will be like is common, and engenders the symptoms known as Fear and Trembling. I assume every new client will have some of it.

I get pretty curious, in fact, if I don't detect a certain amount of F & T in the first meeting. I think outright F & T is a normal reaction to an initial meeting with a shrink-type, don't you? After all, the new client has usually had any number of fantasy meetings with me already, each one scarier than the last. Even if I weren't good at the "I'm-OK, You're-OK" stuff the real meeting would just about have to be a breeze compared to the ones he made up in the car on the way to my office. (A note here - on the streets, any mental health type is called a "shrink." Bob Goulding, MD, advocates using the more positive term "expander," with good reason, and I still prefer "shrink." As in helping folks shrink the Monsters in their lives...)

Of course, I am not supposed to be experiencing F & T prior to the first interview, (even though it's likely I will have had a few meetings in my head with the new person, too), because I have been to Therapy School. In truth, I have done my share of trembulation over the years, whenever I made the new client into an intimidating VIP of some sort in my mind. I still do that occasionally.

Anyhow, here I am turning the handle of the waiting room door, about to meet someone and get fairly intimate with him in the next hour. On the basis of what goes on then (in each of our heads, as well as out in the air between us) we will decide whether we will work together to accomplish the client's therapeutic goals; whether we will become exceedingly close for the next few months or years.

I've been told that the therapeutic relationship is the most important one in the client's life at the time. (Yes, it was a therapist who told me, psychoanalytically oriented, at that - you know, Freudian). Still, I know from experience that this can be true at some times for clients, so opening that door is a pretty big deal. A responsibility like that could call up a little F & T, even if I am the one who's been to Therapy School. Maybe it should.

If this new person and I decide to form a therapeutic team, we'll be doing our own relationship dances, which will in some ways reflect the ones she's doing out there in the world. Choreographed in childhood, repeated performances. Some of the same stuff that brought her into therapy will rear its ugly head in our relationship too. That's fine. It's expected and gives us grist for the therapeutic mill. The deal is to keep my family dances out of the relationship as far as possible, or at least to know when I'm doing those familiar steps and change the lead or the music, if necessary.

So each of us is trying to answer important questions in that first hour while we're talking about his impending divorce, the loss of her job, his early school experiences or her new parenting problems. "Are this person's issues something I know how to deal with?" "Does this therapist seem to get what I'm trying to tell her?" "Will he stick around long enough to make his changes?" "Does she know what the heck she's talking about?" "Am I moving too fast?" "Can I trust her?" "Will we get along well enough to make this work?" "Is she going to judge me?" "Shall we dance...?"

If all goes well, we take the floor for the first set. Each of us has decided, at least tentatively, that we can be partners for a time. And like all partnerships I know of, there are multiple reasons why we've chosen each other, some good, some not so hot. Some we're aware of, some we aren't. First, the "good" reasons. We see in the other a being who's genuine, likeable, motivated, capable, and has potential. Is probably trainable.

Some of you may object to the word "trainable." Well, come on, do you really think we don't train others how to relate to us? Of course we do. And they train us. And this process continues throughout the relationship. With respect, naturally, and loving humor, hopefully - it's easier that way. (Anyhow, I like the term training, and it's my book.)

Do not confuse "training" with making people change. The former is easy and desirable, the latter, impossible. Believe me, I know. Occasionally I forget myself and try to make someone in my practice or in my family change (for their own good, of course). I invariably get my come-uppance. Reciprocal training is more like learning to get along with people, the sort of stuff Bob Fulghum writes about in "All I Really Need to Know I Learned in Kindergarten." (1988, New York; Villard Press) OK, so we're aware that the other seems promising and Good Enough to take a chance on.

Here's a simple example of client-therapist mutual training. He comes in and begins to tell me his story. I try to understand from this just what his world is like. I check out my impressions, he confirms or corrects. I invite him to see things a little differently; he accepts or resists my suggestion. I pay attention. And so on.

And then there are the "bad" reasons we've chosen each other. The unaware reasons, the hidden agendas. Each of us also chooses the pairing because it fits our script expectations in some way. What the heck are script expectations? Well, they comprise the whole set of impressions, beliefs, conclusions, etc, that we formed as kids about life. It's like this - here we are in the years before school busily going about kid business. Playing, fighting, eating, exploring, having chicken pox, making stuff, and being trained.

Meanwhile, our kid lives are full of variables. Our parents like us or they don't (usually some of each); they like each other or they don't (ditto); they enjoy life or they don't (etc); they like other people or they don't (you get the picture). Plus we and our families are subject to the vicissitudes of weather, politics, health, economics, and so on. The upshot is that as kids we go through a mix of painful and pleasant experiences. No one may be at fault for them, but these incidents still affect us.

How we respond to these experiences determines our reality. That is, what we conclude about ourselves, about others and about life forms a filter through which we interpret and understand subsequent events. It's part of how we give meaning to living. Here's the way it works. If our folks' eyes generally lit up when we came in the room, we likely formed a base of positive self-regard from which to conduct our lives. ("I'm OK") If they were pretty squared away (see "To live in this world and be satisfied....") and didn't have major catastrophes to cope with, they probably did a Good Enough parenting job and we grew up planning to like and relate well to most people. ("You're OK")

But what if we had meningitis, or lost a parent, or there was a famine, or we were badly burned, or we were interned in a relocation camp, or there was a major depression? Not to mention what if we were deliberately hurt or neglected by important others, parental units, perhaps? Clearly, if we had to deal with one of the above, we are going to expect different treatment from others, expect to have different emotions, expect to have different physical sensations, and we will learn to see ourselves very differently in all kinds of dimensions than if we were more fortunate.

For a very young child, feeling bad can't be differentiated from being bad. Sobering thought. Early physical and emotional discomfort is part of the foundation for self-badness. In sum, the more unpleasantness we go through as kids, the less likely we are to grow up thinking well of ourselves and others.

So, as youngsters we may conclude all sorts of inaccurate and unuseful things. Like "People I love will hit me." "I must deserve it." "That's life." "In order to get along in the world I'll always have to please others." "Life is a struggle." "Problems can't be solved." "Everyone leaves." "I should know what others want without their having to tell me. If I don't, I'm bad." "If I can keep Mom happy things will be safe." "If Dad's mad, it's my fault." "Being grown-up is no fun." "Being little is dangerous." These are just a few examples of the sorts of beliefs that children may develop in response to early trauma. The beliefs always make sense in the context of our childhoods.

Trouble is, these perceptions are based on a very small sample of human experience. No one's family of origin or early encounters can possibly represent life accurately. But the more traumatic our early years were, the more tightly we hold on to these beliefs, because survival depends on knowing the "truth" about reality: knowing what to expect and how to behave in order to get along in this world.

So even if this early frame of reference dictates some pretty unpleasant beliefs, even if it keeps us in a pretty uncomfortable world, we still cling to it on an unaware level. We notice and give credence to events that support it and discount those that don't. We may even, without consciously intending to, seek out people to relate to who fit our unconscious cast of characters. People who treat us as we really expect, or as we think we deserve.

In no way does this mean we want to keep fulfilling our worst expectations. It's popular to say that some people just want to feel bad. That has never made any sense to me. It's a dumb idea. It invites people who are already hurting because they are in an unsatisfactory situation to beat up on themselves for being there. Phooey! That attitude does not promote change.

I believe people make sense. If they don't seem to, it's just because we lack sufficient information to understand them. (That's one good use for therapeutic nosiness.) Being invested in preserving one's reality is not the same as wanting it. In fact, that's a good way to think about the internal conflict folks experience that helps bring them into therapy. "I don't want it, but I keep doing it." Or on a more helpless level, "Why does this keep happening to me?"

It's easy to imagine that a new client driving to his first Peg-appointment might be experiencing this sort of internal conflict. "I'm in this unpleasant fix, and I'm mad at myself for being there. What's wrong with me?" If he is having this dialogue in his head, he likely expects me to see him as some kind of nitwit too. For example, I once began an interview with a new client who seemed very likeable. I was enjoying getting to know him and being curious about how to help him and was feeling pretty positive and optimistic about the prospect.

As he talked on, he began to look rather sad, and I asked him about that. "I'm picking up all this disapproval from you," he said. Huh? It was sure news to me that I felt disapproving, and I said so. Since he had been talking about having very critical and disapproving parents, I asked if he might be getting me mixed up with them. "Oh no," he replied, "I used to do that, but I'm all over that now..." Oh well, you can't win 'em all.

Or maybe I am being pictured as some sort of guru who will have all the answers. Or as untrustworthy, someone who will let him down in familiar ways, reproducing familiar hurts. Or all of the above. I call this process having the relationship in your head. We all do it, even those of us who have been to Therapy School. Hopefully, us shrink-types will be more aware of doing it and keep it in perspective. Hopefully. Therapy School calls these fantasy processes Transference (if it's theirs) and Counter-transference (if it's ours).

Starting to dance is getting more and more complicated, isn't it? And more interesting, if you happen to be curious about how things work, like I am. That curiosity is part of why I chose Therapy School in the first place. One of the better reasons. One of the aware reasons.

At any rate, we each start out, on our respective sides of the couch, relating to someone who isn't, strictly speaking, actually sitting there, but who is partly a fiction. An antique. A "filament" of our imagination... And we tend to notice the aspects of the interaction that support these distortions and not notice those that challenge them. Or at least not credit that data as much. So no matter what we're talking about, divorces or jobs or scares or hopes or embarrassments or successes or cabbages or kings, we are meanwhile peeling away the layers of fantasy we've pasted on the other, without realizing we'd done that. Gives real meaning to the phrase "getting to know you…"

You can understand from all this that my life dances will differ from yours because they were learned in different childhoods - different worlds, in effect. Our choreography was governed by this concern, "How do I have to be, how do I have to act, what do I have to do to get along in this family?" What worked in one family certainly wouldn't in another. Some of us learned some pretty darned tricky moves to negotiate the home dance floor and please the grown-up instructors. Maybe a bit complicated for our little feet. We learned, though, and the more important the performances were, the more we hang on the routine as adults, not noticing that the stage, cast, and audience have changed.

You can think of these dances as part of the Script we each wrote for ourselves as kids. How our lives would go. The script is out of date, however, and needs revising in light of current events. Will it play in Peoria? Probably not, since we wrote the bulk of it in early childhood, when our ability to understand and explain things was that of a pre-schooler. Very referential. That is, we experienced events as directed at us or because of us when they weren't. But we didn't know that, and therefore felt guilty and confused about many things we had no responsibility for. Like a parent's misery, or a death, or a divorce, or violence.

Further, a child is quite grandiose in his thinking. His ego boundaries are not yet well developed. If he still thinks he's the center of the universe, he probably sees his impact as bigger than it really is. Cause and effect are often very magical. "Step on a crack…" He believes in mind reading, and he sees things in black and white. As good or bad - period.

Options for coping and problem solving (the dance steps) are age-limited too. Most of them boil down to some form of being good. Or sometimes being bad. And even sometimes being gone. Not existing, figuratively or literally. So a script may have a tragic ending. The adult that this child turns into may not figure out that he has more effective and powerful options now, if he is still reading from the dog-eared pages of this childhood drama. This fairy tale. So, for example, he may try to please everyone else when there's conflict, even when that approach is absolutely inappropriate, say at work, or with his kids.

It's this early way of viewing things, this early childhood frame of reference, that is probably interfering with living in this world and being satisfied, and being happy with self and others. After all, the grown-up part of us knows very well how to structure our lives successfully. But without realizing it, we may let the kid part of us with this young frame of reference run the show at times when that's not such a hot idea. Especially when we're under stress. Especially if that stress echoes old familiar dilemmas.

For example, everyone ends relationships in their lives. It's part of living. If, as kids, we experienced some form of important loss, such as a parental divorce, we are likely to react to the loss of a relationship in our adult lives in much the same way as we responded to our parents' divorce. Like we may have feelings that seem out of proportion to the present separation. Or we may have trouble getting on with ending the relationship, even though it's what we want and know is best for us. Or we may believe that we are somehow Bad, as kids often do in a divorce, even though we know in our grown-up part that this is hooey.

It's sort of like the old experience is pasted on top of the current one, only we usually aren't aware of that. So we're trying to solve two problems at once, which is much harder than taking one at a time. Particularly when one of them is unsolvable, since it's over and done with. Yet maybe the kid part of us is still trying to keep our parents together in the past by not going ahead with the present break-up.

Or maybe if we put off the separation, we won't have to feel all of those awful hurts we felt as kids during that loss, and which are now rearing their ugly heads.

So the kid part of us may, in effect, be preventing the adult part from problem-solving. One of the reasons nature made shrinks is to help clients unpaste the old business from the current business and live happier ever after.

Believing in self-badness interferes significantly with having a good time and living happily ever after. So does believing in other-badness. But there's usually a fair sprinkling of both beliefs in a person's script because of that black and white thinking, and because none of us had a perfect childhood.

The situation is further complicated by the coexistence of an entirely different frame of reference in the grown-up part of us; the reality-testing part of us that does live in this world. That does see most things in shades of grey, and does know that we and others are pretty OK in general, though we may not always behave in an exemplary fashion.

You know, we wouldn't want everything we've done published in the evening Tribune...but we're basically nice folks who have a right to be in the human race. And it's this way of looking at things that we are most aware of. So we can't figure out why we sometimes feel so bad about ourselves, or are so lonely, or are Flunking Relationships. And then we may harass ourselves about that. Yech!

What this boils down to is that a person comes to therapy expecting two very different experiences. At least two. On a grown up, aware, level she imagines that since I have been to Therapy School I will be helpful, interested, competent, non-judgmental, skilled, etc. The younger, less aware, part of her, however, figures I'll probably be just like all the others. The important figures from her past who have taken care of her or have let her down one way or another.

As the one on the therapist side of the couch, it's my job to be aware that these conflicting expectations exist for everyone, and that that conflict has something to do with why the client is sitting in my office today on the other side of the couch. So I strive to ally all parts of me with the parts of her that want to change her life course.

Together, the team we form should provide enough strength and protection to make it safe to give up the early script beliefs that have gotten her through so far, but are in her way now. A script re-write. Most everyone enters therapy to stop doing the things they did to make it through childhood. Naturally, that's not such an easy process. Clients will say "But changing is so hard." And I will say "Not nearly as hard as what you have been doing - not nearly as hard as not changing has been on you."

One man said "I opened the cupboard, and all the cans said 'worms'." Yup, it looks that way at times. So we just take one can at a time. At the client's own pace. He's in charge. (Remember what I said earlier about Making People Change) No question about it. We're training each other. He's teaching me how to help him. Not necessarily to always do what they said to do in Therapy School, but what works with him. I'm teaching him how to Live in this world...etc. And how to use me to best advantage. As we Get to Know each other the script fantasies diminish. We begin to see who's really sitting on the other side of the couch. Working through the transference. Now we can really cut a rug together!

How does this work, anyhow? Well, at the same time that we are talking about, say, how to communicate more effectively with the boss, we are modeling that same kind of communication with each other. Nifty, huh? Practice what you preach. It sure wouldn't make much sense to be encouraging a client to be nurturing to herself or to someone else if I treated her in a judgmental way myself. Or if she could sense that I never give myself any slack. You gotta be the real

McCoy. Not perfect, but Good Enough to have a relationship with the client that is sincerely positive. Happy with self and other. You teach it, you model it. (Now you know one reason I've spent a lot of time on the client side of the couch.)

The relationship is the main tool for change. Most clients don't suspect that they've come in to train me so that we can dance well together. They think they're in the client chair to decide whether to get a divorce, or to be more assertive, or to stop being anxious. And so they are. Using the therapeutic alliance to accomplish that.

I'd like to say a few words about the therapeutic alliance. No, that's not true, I'd actually like to say a great many words about the therapeutic alliance - it's one of my favorite subjects. It gets a lot of coverage in Therapy School. Trouble is, there's an impressive amount of disagreement on exactly what it should look like.

The professors in a certain branch of Therapy School, for example, tell you the therapeutic relationship must exist in one room only, between, say, 4:00 and 4:50 on Tuesday afternoons, and the therapist must appear to go into hibernation between meetings. Must give no hint that she has any other reason for living than to spring alive at 3:59 pm each Tuesday to meet with the client for that hour. Actually, for that 50 minutes. Not 49 or 51. Must not reveal herself as a human being in any way. I believe that the idea behind all this is that the therapist will be putting no personal input into the relationship and that therefore all of how the client experiences the partnership will be made up of his transference distortions, which can then be analyzed for neurotic content. ("Neurotic" is a more expensive way to say self-badness.)

I've also never figured out how one could bring this off. Have all therapy offices decorated exactly the same? Require therapist uniforms? What if the therapist had onions for lunch? Or got a different hairdo? Or new squeaky shoes? How could one avoid injecting something of oneself into the relationship? I don't get it.

At the opposite end of the spectrum, some other Therapy School professors say that the therapist and client should contract for the therapist to be very prominent in the relationship. Be the client's new parent. The original parental units must have screwed up, so he needs to be re-parented. I haven't figured out this one either, but I do know that it gives me moderate F & T.

So anyhow, whatever you were taught in T.S. about dancing becomes still another influence on the relationship. A conscious one, mostly. But wait, there's more. As if all these aware and not-so-aware personal factors shaping the therapeutic partnership weren't enough, there are cultural factors to keep in mind as well. Sheese!

I'll give an example of what I mean. I've led a couple dozen workshops for folks in human services on preventing burn-out. As part of these, I have asked participants (nurses, counselors, teachers, administrators, etc.) to free-associate to two terms. The first term represented their role. "Nurse," for example. The second, the population they served. "Patient," in this case. Regardless of job title, the associations to the "helping" role always look about the same - "smart, caring, responsible, tired, capable, hardworking..." always. So do the associations to the "helped" role - "needy, stuck, hurting, demanding, victim, stubborn..." and so on.

There are other associations, of course, but the bulk of them describe the "helper" as with-it, together, and good at problem-solving. There is little or no mention of personal needs or feelings for these folks. The "helpee," in contrast, is pictured as having big hurts and as needing a lot of help and nurturing, because he's not very good at doing that for himself.

It doesn't matter who makes up the audience. I would get the same responses from your aerobics class if I asked them. Because these represent cultural stereotypes. Images we call up when we envision these roles. We were raised with them and we all have them, just as we all have racial stereotypes. Even though we may not act on them.

The tricky part is this. As with the individual's script beliefs, these shared stereotypes coexist, more or less out of sight, with the part of us that knows better. Like background noise. If our reality-testing part is functioning pretty well, the noise won't get to us. We'll act out of rational understanding, not prejudice or kid beliefs. But it's still there. And has the potential to really affect how we dance, if we're not on our toes...

There's another twist, too. Script frames of reference are individual. "Yours is green, mines is orange," as Bill Cosby says in one of his locker room routines. Not so with these role stereotypes. They are shared. The human on each side of the couch grew up encountering them on TV, at school, in comics, at church, and so on. In their oatmeal, so to speak.

So before they ever meet, both parties share a view of how these two folks will get along. How they will dance. These associations feature the shrink as Big Person and the client as Little Person. The Problem-solver and the Problem-solvee. Or perhaps the Helpful and the Helpless. Or in reverse, maybe the Needy and the Need-less. That doesn't mean that either party intends it or wants it, but just that this set-up seems right and proper to a part of both of them. They can easily cooperate in setting it up - unknowingly.

Like how? Like either of them seeing the client as fragile. Fragile? Hornswaggle! The worse trauma a person has survived in her life, the tougher she is. If she's not dead or crazy she figured out how to get through the trauma and is therefore smart and tough. It's a great disservice to approach her any other way. She merits applause, not kid gloves. A Polka, in celebration!

Being appropriately gentle and sensitive is very different from the disrespect of walking on eggs around the client. Hard to imagine doing the Polka on eggshells... It's all too popular to portray the client as permanently disabled by early trauma. Fiddlesticks! Much more often it's the therapist who isn't tough enough. (An aside here: I work only with adults. A lot of these assumptions don't apply with kid clients, so keep that in mind. I'm not brave enough for that kind of work and admire my colleagues who are.)

You can't celebrate client power in a Big Person - Little Person relationship. So you can't sell him short by doing most of the thinking in the partnership. Even if he acts like he can't. Especially if he acts like he can't. Or by putting more energy into problem-solving than he is. Or being more uncomfortable with his stuckness than he is. Or by reducing fees inappropriately. Or by seeing him as helpless and not expecting hard things of him. These are all ways to perpetuate self-badness, not cure it.

Of course a few folks have total grievance recall. Betty MacDonald, in her delightful book, "The Plague and I," referred to them as Big Saddos. Some therapists think they are enhancing the therapeutic alliance by supporting such a client's black and white view of his life. Heroes and villains. It doesn't work to spend your time helping the client Gather Evidence for other-badness. This is another way to sell the client short, because he's still regarding himself as a Victim. (Remember, people-badness is "bad think" - doesn't promote Living in this World, etc.) Many folks were victimized as children. They can get over the effects of that, but not as long as they continue to operate as Victims now. Get it?

Some clients, on the other hand, have insufficient grievance recall. They need to get better at it. The therapist, naturally, must know how to tell the difference and what to do about it.

In order to avoid the presumptuousness of a Big Person - Little Person dance, the therapist must support success, not suffering. Even if it means being accused of Not Understanding. Or Not Caring. Helping professionals as a group tend to be much too vulnerable to complaints that they are not being helpful enough, and have to learn not to be invested in being seen as grown-up boy scouts, always kind, courteous & helpful. A shrink (or a parent) who can't stand to be viewed as hard-nosed is sunk. Might as well turn in your helper badge.

Dr. Z., one of my Therapy School professors, gave a great example of this kind of potency. He said that no teacher was worth her salt if she couldn't freeze a kid at 30 paces with a glance. I've always loved that image, and use it a lot as an illustration with clients.

But boy, is this hard to learn! Because most of us helpful sorts learned that helpful role as kids in our family dances. So we have the sense that our Place in Heaven depends on pleasing or taking care of others. The rational part of us knows better, but the cultural pressures and the script expectations mesh and may carry the day. Double whammy! I've spent a lot of my time on the client side of the couch learning to be Unreasonable. Learning the value of making waves and being not especially helpful. Learning to not try so hard. As I learn, I have way more fun and am much more effective!

This Big Person - Little Person stuff can be kind of subtle. Just when I'm privately patting myself on the back for being willing to negotiate a lower fee for someone because he's in Dire Straits, he may show up in his brand new BMW... Oh well, more grist for the mill. Chances are, this person came to see me in the first place because he couldn't figure out why folks in his life kept getting so mad at him.

There's an essential point here. That is, that neither party can create a BP - LP relationship by herself; there has to be a secret agreement to do it. It is not something you can do to someone else, any more than you can make a dance partner follow your lead. (Remember the part about Making People Change.) I can act as clever and capable as I want, and I can't keep the client from being just as potent. From solving the therapeutic dilemmas as well as (or better than) I. Likewise, the client can present herself as virtually helpless because that's her reality, and she still can't make me buy into that by taking over responsibility for her progress.

I stress this point mainly to undercut Therapist Guilt. When I talk about BP - LP relating to therapists, many of them start the self-badness tapes running in their heads. "Oh my gosh, I'm re-victimizing the client. What about my Place in Heaven?" So I reassure them that this behavior is not a Sin, it's merely doing the dance steps that they learned as kids. They don't have to Confess and self-flagellate, they can just change the music. And how about if they pay some attention to the ways in which playing the Big Person role sells them short, instead of only paying attention to how they may have been discounting the client?

How, in trying very hard to be a Good Therapist they may have not given themselves any room to be whole persons in their relationships. To have wants and feelings that get taken into account too, just as the client's do. Not "either-or;" "both-and." In my experience, prolonged Big Personism engenders some strong emotions in the theraperson. Resentment. Exhaustion. Feeling unappreciated. And guilt about these feelings. If the therapist starts feeling like she can't look another client in the face, she might consider whether she's trying to be Super Shrink, the heroine who rights all the wrongs in the world.

Some T.S. students turn the stuff they were taught into Gospel. Getting along in their families probably depended on their being Good Kids, Helpful variety. Selfless. And it hasn't come to their attention that they've grown up and moved out and don't have to be that way any more. The audience and cast have changed. So here's the client on her side of the couch trying to get rid of self-badness, never suspecting that the therapist on the other side may be doing same. Actually, neither of them suspecting. Hmmm.

What to do? Wait. I believe I hear the Author's Message coming up here... Have a regular relationship. No, no, I'm not saying the therapist should become just another, more expensive, buddy. What would be the point? I'm only suggesting that the therapist keep focused on the forest, not the trees. That she keep in mind the reasons behind those Therapy School teachings about how to dance. They are mostly quite sensible, established as guidelines to help you be effective as a therapist, not as measures of your OKness. Nor are they there to help you keep your humanity from showing.

You've just read about the personal and cultural influences on the therapeutic partnership. I'm sure you can see how they often act together to make it tough not to have a Big and Little person relationship. And I'm sure you can also see how impossible it would be to try to teach Living in this World with Satisfaction, and Being Happy with Self and Others in the context of a relationship that didn't reflect that. ATTENTION! DOUBLE MESSAGE, DOUBLE MESSAGE! Remember, the relationship is the tool for change.

So what does a regular, I'm-OK - You're-OK therapeutic relationship look like? Well, it looks like any I+ - Y+ relationship, with some different boundaries. It doesn't much look like I thought in T.S. that it would. It doesn't look very solemn, for instance. Somehow I got the idea that it was disrespectful not to be solemn. I've been doing this stuff since 1974 and have yet to find any evidence that people change their lives faster if they are more solemn. Or that the work counts more if you do it that way.

My label for this misconception is The Merthiolate Syndrome. You know, "If it doesn't hurt, it's not doing you any good." (Or its corollary, "If it tastes bad, it must be good for you"). Hogwash! Read Norman Cousins if you don't believe me.(9) While you're at it, you could read Eric Berne and Milton Erickson too.(3)(14) I wonder how things might be different if Bactine had been invented before Freud was...

And the therapeutic relationship doesn't look very reverent, either. Reverent, yawn... What the heck does reverence have to do with getting someone to want to dance with you? Personally, I would be suspicious of anyone who proposed to teach me how to be happier in the world but who took herself so seriously that she wouldn't laugh at herself, and at life. Or who saw me as too fragile to call bullpucky on. Or who didn't obviously get a real kick out of her work.

The monsters in our lives can't survive being poked fun at. They derive their power from being Too Terrible to look at, think about, talk about, or especially to laugh at. Take the Early Abuse monsters, for instance. Some of them are truly dreadful. They represent enormous betrayals of trust through torture, neglect, incest, even attempted murder. The conclusions a child draws about self, others, and life following such experiences are, as you can imagine, awful. It may be almost impossible to envision her letting go of those tightly held beliefs, her reality, and making the leap to being happy with self and others as an adult. She may not believe she can do it.

It's easy to understand wanting to tiptoe around such an adult survivor. Wanting to protect her from any further pain. Fearing that she might easily crack and fall to pieces if you said the wrong thing. And yet you, as therapist, won't do her a darned bit of good if you too start seeing this trauma as overwhelming. So you'd better believe she has guts and brains enough to learn to spit in the face of Early Abuse Monsters.

So I say to folks "You gotta have coffidence." No, not confidence, coffidence. I tell them about the time husband Ragnar and I were playing pool at a local tavern. At the pool table next to us wavered a guy who was, as they say, "drunker'n a skunk." Barely ambulatory. But intent on his game, even though he was losing badly. Neither of us will ever forget the moment when he turned to us after another lousy shot, winked, belched, and said, "Ya gotta have coffidence!"

Now if someone can't imagine a therapist telling a story like that to an incest survivor when she's feeling doubtful of ever seeing the light at the end of the tunnel, he may be suffering from an unhealthy solemnity blood level and should consult his physician. Or worse, he could be Humor Impaired. Humor impairment isn't fatal - just deadly - but it prevents Satisfaction and Happiness with Self and Others and, therefore, should receive immediate attention at the nearest treatment center.

One of the most important things a therapist has to offer is hope. Telling an anecdote like this is one of the ways I share with the client my unwavering hope. My coffidence in her, in me, in the process, and in humanity in general. I can express this in a sober and straightforward fashion too, but I try to avoid doing so if there's any way we can have fun at it.

So an effective therapeutic relationship has all of the elements of any positive relationship in a person's life. Respect, caring, playing, working, goofing around, conflict, exasperation, frustration, give and take, commitment, joy, sorrow, trust, anger, fear, guilt, and existential absurdity. It endures through all of these, as well as through life's milestones - births, deaths, graduations, marriages and divorces.

What makes it different from being buddies is the contract. We are doing all this for one purpose only - to help the client achieve his therapeutic goals. That's what he's paying his dough for. The boundaries defining this kind of relationship exist to promote achievement of that goal: whatever piece of Pat's statement he isn't accomplishing.

That's why we're going to all the trouble to train each other. We're together to problem-solve, not to be friends, but unless we become friends, the process won't work. Here is one of the paradoxes I mentioned earlier. As one of my students says, "It's enough to make your brains ache."

As if all of the above weren't complicated enough, the therapist needs to be aware that as she and her client get better and better at dancing together, the relationship evolves. So that while she may have been elevated by the client initially to a position of power and potency by, the client eventually turns her into more of a colleague; useful, but not necessary. This is one of the indications that therapy is in its final stages. It goes without saying that the theraperson should do whatever she can to facilitate this re-ownership of power by the client. Pedestals are pretty darned shaky places to hang out.

In sum, I've done what most shrinks do: understood that all branches of T.S. have something to teach about the therapeutic relationship. And then figured out in the trenches what the heck I think therapeutic relating really amounts to. Whether with this particular partner at this particular moment it's going to be a Tango or Western Swing. In any case, we're going to have a pretty darned good time while we're at it.

CHAPTER 2

Essential Technical Vocabulary
(that they don't teach you-know-where...)

Big, Important, words abound in Therapy School. In spite of this, I've noticed that they fail to teach a number of technical terms that I have found essential to my work. To correct this oversight, I've included some of these terms here for your use and enjoyment.

BRAIN DEAD - A more fun way to say "I stopped thinking." Brain death is a common child response to situations that would make her feel crazy if she thought about them. Makes sense for a kid with relatively few options, but Brain Aliveness works much better for adults.

ONE MAN AWAY FROM WELFARE - The condition of many women in our culture. I read it in Ms. Magazine many years ago and couldn't forget it. I use it in various contexts, but mostly when I'm working with a female client on issues of economic self-sufficiency. It gets the point across.

PLACE IN HEAVEN - A lovely phrase borrowed from Peg Bracken, who wrote the "I Hate to Housekeep" book. It's marvelous for putting things in perspective. She used the phrase to help the housekeeper set priorities, as in "Will failure to make your bed lose you your place in heaven?" Thank you, Peg, for your permissions to me when I was an innocent young bride and still took housekeeping seriously.

My friends have been a big help to me here, too. One time one of them said, "Oh yeah, I know it's time to wash the kitchen floor when my socks stick and pull off." I'd say I'm at least that compulsive. In fact, I have a sign on my fridge (and on my office bulletin board too) which reads "Dull Women Have Immaculate Homes." Like it? Help yourself.

MY HEAD IS TOO FULL - The condition humans get into when trying to keep too many balls in the air at once. Symptoms include leaving the faucet running in the sink, letting pots boil dry, forgetting to pick up the dry cleaning, etc. You're familiar with the state, I'm sure.

The reason I bring it up is to point out that it is a normal occurrence from time to time, not a character flaw. Some folks give themselves no slack, even though they are in charge of the PTA fund-raiser, the kids have chicken-pox, and it's the week before Christmas. "Get off your own case," I say, "your head is just too full and some stuff is leaking out. No big deal." Besides, a friend of mine made it up years ago and I think it's cute.

BUILDING CHARACTER (see Merthiolate Syndrome) - Most of the folks I work for (my clients) suffer from having done way too much of this in service of eradicating self-badness. When they enter therapy, they expect it to be yet another Character Building experience - awful, but Good For Them. So they are willing to endure all sorts of discomfort if it will make them better. They are surprised to find that I do just about everything in my power to teach them the virtues of having less character and more fun. In fact, we often have quite a struggle about this for a while.

JOIN THE HUMAN RACE - What some clients hope to be able to do once they have Built Sufficient Character. Meanwhile, they treat themselves as if they don't deserve a spot there.

OOPS - This is a magic word. It was given to me by Dr. Z while I was in one of his training groups. See, I was having a fit of self-badness. These attacks were frequent in those days, and I mainly dealt with them by extensive self-flagellation. BORING. Caught up in the awfulness of it all, however, I didn't have this perspective. Dr. Z was a great help to me when he broke into one of my self-punishing monologues saying, "Would you like to know a magic word to use instead of all these others from now on when you do something wrong?" Desperately, I answered, "Oh, yes, please!"

After a dramatic pause (Dr. Z is very good at dramatic pauses) he said, "Oops." Although lacking the tragic quality of my usual responses to mistakes, "oops" is certainly more efficient. So I pass it along to clients when they begin to get out their whips and hair shirts, giving proper credit to the source, of course.

TWITTERPATED - One of my favorites - I hope it will become one of yours. I'm surprised at how few people are familiar with Twitterpation. Didn't they read Bambi? It's what the animals do in pairs in the spring. You know, the butterflies, and the bunnies and all the rest.

And "twitterpated" avoids all the pitfalls of LOVE. When someone comes in looking all goofy and grinning because they've met a new honey, I can say, "Girl, are you Twitterpated?" She doesn't have to evaluate the precise nature of her feelings the way she might if I mentioned LOVE, and can give a simple answer. People who are Twitterpated definitely need things kept simple for them, you know. Thanks, Walt Disney, we needed that.

DOUGH - Years ago, Eric Berne wrote that people in therapy groups would talk much more easily about sex than about money. This holds true for many professors in T.S. too. It's almost like it's bad manners to refer to the fact that our clients support us with their payments. Like we ought to pretend we're doing this for love or something. It's amazing how hard it is for some of us helper-types to ask for money. Since clients don't want to talk about it publicly and neither do therapists, where does that leave us? With something very important not being talked about, that's where. Just like a dysfunctional family. Heaven forbid! So in order to bring this elephant out from under the rug, I started calling it dough. Works great. "Gimme your dough." "Let's talk about dough." If they are in arrears, "Help, where's my dough?" If a group member wants to negotiate fees, I always do that in the group setting. Brings up all sorts of interesting stuff for everyone, including me.

TRUTH POLICE - Another wonderful client invention. Therapy School really needed a catchy term for folks who get themselves in trouble by insisting on being Right. Here's how it came up. I was working with a client whose therapeutic contract was to get along better with people. She was telling of how she got fired after pointing out how her boss was wrong about something. In front of co-workers, no less. So I asked her how come it was her job to correct him. She thought hard. All of a sudden she smiled brightly and said, "I know, I'm the Truth Police!" She Got it. And so has everyone else I've used it with since. You can vary this term as needed: for example, Thought Police, Mother Police, Therapy Police, the possibilities are endless.

KID WAYS TO SAY IT BETTER - This category includes stuff like the bronx cheer, phooey, baloney, oh yeah?, says who?, yippee skippee, dork, poopy, nope, goofy, yuck, icky, uggo, cranky, whiney,etc. It would be sort of silly for me to give a long sermon on why kid words work better most of the time than loooong, Important ones. In fact, when I'm working and deem it absolutely necessary to use an Important word, I usually excuse myself by saying that I'm just doing it so the client will know she got her money's worth that meeting.

Kid words demystify, puncture grandiosity, deflate people-badness, get the client's attention, and are more fun. I use 'em and I teach clients to use 'em. Feel free to add your own.

ANTS AND GRASSHOPPERS - Another issue that people get into their corners about is proper money handling. There's no problem-solving as long as your beliefs about dough make you Right or Wrong. So I bring in the diagnostic aid of Aesop's fable about the ants and the grasshopper. (Courtesy of Walt Disney) Remember, the ants worked hard all summer putting away supplies for the winter, while the grasshopper laughed at them and fiddled the season away. You guessed it, come the snows he was begging at their door for handouts.

People know immediately which of the two bugs they are. And their partner is. If they're having heavy conflict around dough, they are probably one of each. Two ants or two grasshoppers usually don't fight a lot about money, but they either may not have much fun or may not have a secure retirement, depending. With a mixed marriage, I point out that the other's approach is valuable, not a character flaw, and that they have much to learn from one another. And that both ants and grasshoppers deserve a place in heaven.

OH WELL... - An excellent response to Righteous or Moralistic "gotchas." Example: "I thought you were a better person than that, Zenobia; you've really disappointed me!" Instead of trying to convince this VIP that you deserve a place in the human race, I suggest, "Oh well.." After a little practice you can add a slight lift of the eyebrows, shoulder shrug, and upraised palms. Very effective at extinguishing such rudeness.

IMPAIRED or *DISABLED* - Garrison Keillor once featured a guest on his radio show who described himself as "singing-impaired," and even slightly "dancing-impaired." For me, this phrase presented a super way to spoof self- and other-badness. So now if a client making a case for other-badness out of his partner's failure to offer him enough positive strokes, I may say, "Maybe she's stroking-impaired, and just needs to be trained. Lots of folks in our culture have stroking disabilities." Once the behavior is re-framed from being a character flaw into merely a lack of social skill, the badness is peeled off and it can be approached with creative kid problem-solving.

DANCE - A technical term for relationship. Brings nice images to mind, and takes some of the heaviness out of Relating. Especially important when both partners are shrinks...

IN A DIFFERENT ROOM - A phrase born out of client exasperation with a parental unit. This particular mom evidently doesn't pay much attention to the responses she's eliciting from others, or to what's going on around her. So one time my client was describing a particularly embarrassing scene in a grocery store in which mom was doing her thing and getting weird looks from other shoppers. Client wanted to crawl under the rug. "Ophelia," I said, "your mom was in a different store than the rest of you were. Sometimes she operates in an alternate universe, and it just looks like you're all in the same room. So don't expect her to be any different, and remember that you're not her, so you don't have to be embarrassed by her antics. You could even get a kick out of them." Ophelia followed my advice, and this phrase has become embedded in her group's glossary.

TURNIP - Someone in a client's life who's not likely to give them something they really want. Like altruistic caring, for instance, or approval. The reason for the withholding doesn't really matter; it could be stinginess or ignorance or a Matter of Principle. What's relevant is that this person is not a good candidate to ask for this particular item from, unless you're fond of banging your head against the wall.

Turnip is a less pejorative term than the client is probably currently using for the person in question, so it undercuts people-badness. It also helps shift the question from "why is this so-and-so not responding," to "why keep trying to get blood out of a turnip?" Why not look for a more generous vegetable? I sometimes give clients homework to go buy a turnip and put it on their windowsill. When it starts to smell, they throw it out.

ARCHEOLOGY - Another word for therapeutic nosiness. Only useful if digging around in the dirt unearthing relics from the past will help the client get unstuck in the present.

POPCORN - Very useful term when working with sexual issues. Folks tend to have Great Big Feelings in this arena because of all the meanings they assign to anything having to do with sex. That's why they tell you in Social Skills 101 to avoid this topic, along with religion and politics, at cocktail parties. So a client may say, "I don't want sex as often as he does; I'm afraid there must be something wrong with me. He tells me I'm rejecting him if I don't always want sex when he does. It probably means something bad that I don't necessarily like sex the way he does."

At this point I often ask her to say all that over again, substituting the word popcorn for the word sex. Try it. Sounds different that way doesn't it? Then I propose that they give sexual behavior no more significance than popcornal behavior. After that, it's not hard to negotiate about when to have it, and there are no hurt feelings related to who thinks of it more often, or who likes it better. Of course I could accomplish the same thing with another image. I just happen to love popcorn!

BED DEATH - I heard Merilee Clunis, PhD, use this term at a WSPA conference for Women in Psychology. It's a great label for a condition that is fairly common in relationships, but which no one thinks should ever occur in Theirs. Clients tend to generate Great Big Feelings when it does occur, which makes working creatively with the situation tough. "Bed death," like "popcorn," can help shrink the problem down to manageable proportions. Thanks, Merilee.

SAVE MY PLACE - What I say to clients if I get up to go to the bathroom, or leave the therapy room for any other reason. I have no important psychological reason for doing this, I just think it's nice to let the kid part of them know I'll be back.

HUMPH (also *HUH, HMMM*) - I can't understand why this term was never taught in Therapy School, as it is probably the single most versatile intervention there is. Depending on how it's delivered, "humph" can indicate incredulity, displeasure, laughter, disapproval, silliness, and even agreement. Possibilities are practically endless, especially if you happen to have a goatee...

TACKY - My favorite parental criticism. It's mild enough to use with clients ("That was tacky, Desdimona") and to teach clients to use with others. With practice, can become nearly as versatile as "humph".

RAFFLEFLAX! - An expletive you don't have to delete. I learned it from an old high school boyfriend. I love it and so does everyone I've exposed to it so far.

PARENTAL UNIT - This term has the advantage of being genderless as well as funny. It's from Saturday Night Live originally, I believe. Since everyone's original relationships were with parental units, we spend a lot of time around the couch discussing them.

POLTERGUYS - The guys who do all the stuff we can't explain.

I assume some of you readers know some more technical terms that I haven't included here. Feel free to send them in for the next volume.

CHAPTER 3

Groups, the joy of...

The occasional client comes in requesting group treatment. More typically, I bring up the idea. I'll suggest the possibility of working in a group setting after I'm sure our dance team is a going concern, and when I think that a group experience would be more powerful therapeutically. The usual response is "I'd die first, thank you." (or its variants, "After Hell Freezes Over," and "Two Chances of that, Fat and Slim...") Now this is understandable, if you recall the F & T surrounding starting therapy in the first place. "You've gotta be kidding! You expect me to expose myself all over again, in front of a bunch of strangers? Give me a break, IDF, etc."

We may discuss the idea for months - years, even. Since most clients picture group therapy as some kind of cross between something they've seen on a TV sitcom and a touchy-feely group from the human potential movement, we spend a lot of time talking about what it's really like.

For instance, I often quote the man who described starting group thusly; "I came to my appointment with Peg, and she had invited all these other people." That's what it was like for him - he had to share his time and space. It wasn't until after he had made all these folks his close friends that he understood the power of loving support from a group of people who knew him thoroughly and accepted him as he was. It's much harder to hold onto self-badness in the face of honest feedback from seven friends than in one-to-one therapy. So I can honestly tell clients it's for their own good...

39

I find working with groups exciting and energizing. I love it and I love to teach about it. I am leading one group that's 15 years old. Can you imagine? I hasten to point out that I'm the only one who's been there all that time. Members do graduate. Or flee, occasionally, (there's that old musty script again...)

Groups are great fun, too. Picture this - here's a group with gay and straight members. New person joins and, as usual, doesn't talk too much at first. So after a few weeks, one of the gay men says to the new guy, who is straight, "Say, you're aware that some of us are gay, and I'm wondering how you feel about that."

Now here I am sitting across the room chuckling to myself because I happen to know that this new man has several gay siblings. I can't wait for his reply. So he explains this to the first man, who is taken aback by this information. Hardly missing a beat, however, he looks the straight client full in the face and retorts, "Well, haven't you ever worried that there might be something wrong with you?!" We crack up.

And then there was the group my friend Karen and I led in the basement of the halfway house where we were consulting therapists. In the former coal room, to be exact - it was the most confidential setting I ever worked in - had a metal door about a foot thick. Anyhow, the members were in their early twenties and had all had recent psychiatric hospitalizations. It was labeled the Emancipation Group because its purpose was to help these folks get ready to live on their own in less supported situations. So we were doing a lot of talking about Social Skills.

Now you have to understand my friend Karen. She's pretty loose. So she decided, in context, as I recall, that one of the topics we needed to cover was the social uses of belching and farting. Honest. She was on a roll, and pretty soon was up on one bun pretending to demonstrate farting options. I mean, really! We like to died!

Originally, we had been sitting on big pillows on the floor but by this time were rolling around with tears in our ears, holding our sides and gasping for air. One of the young residents rolled a little closer and asked me, laughing hysterically , "Is this therapy?" "The best kind," I gasped. That group was rechristened the B & F Group, for obvious reasons. They never covered this sort of group in Therapy School, let me tell you.

Another social skill best learned in a group setting is assertiveness. In a good working group members get kind of uppity. Here's an example. Topic was length of time in group. The client with the most tenure announced grandly, "I've been here longest, that makes me Queen of Group." "But wait," I said, "I've been here longer than you, doesn't that make me the Queen?" Someone else piped up with, "No, no, you're only the treasurer..." I don't get no respect.

Learning to use a group to best effect requires self-assertion. In one-to-one therapy, the client doesn't have to do anything but show up to get my undivided attention. In group, though, he has to learn to take personal responsibility for getting the floor. In doing so, he usually runs head-on into the dilemmas that brought him into therapy originally. "How do I get what I want in this room full of people who also want attention?"

Generally, his first strategy is to take whatever role he took in his family and in subsequent groups in his life - scouts, Sunday school, athletic teams, and so on. So he may be very helpful to others. Or a clown. Or a rebel. Or even a scapegoat. He'll get attention for each of these, but probably won't find it satisfying.

Eventually, he gives up his competitive view of group. "Let's see, group is two hours long and there are eight of us, so that means I'm entitled to 15 minutes. Or 17.14 if someone's absent..." Sounds pretty skimpy, doesn't it? Fortunately, that's not how it works. Members learn that they can take the entire two hours if they really seem to need it, and that others are happy to have them do it. And that they can expect their fellow members to be honest with them. Expect that others won't just defer to be polite and then resent it. And that if they do, that truly is their own problem.

Group is the perfect setting for working the kinks out of Pat's statement. A client can start out protesting that members' feelings for her are merely a pose - "the way we're supposed to treat each other in here." If she sticks around long enough, however, she inevitably surrenders her self-badness in the face of superior numbers.

I don't mean that it's all roses and sunshine. We each have sides to us that we're not aware of. But other people are. And in group the contract includes informing others of what we're seeing about them that they aren't. How rude. This feedback, being unsolicited, can be disconcerting, to say the least. Even if it's positive, but especially if it seems negative to the person in the spotlight.

He may feel old familiar feelings of embarrassment and even shame. Awful feelings. Like he's been exposed doing something very bad. This reaction makes sense, since that aspect of him may have been unacceptable in childhood, leading him to learn to hide it from himself. To disown it - "that's not me." Group members function as loving mirrors which reflect disowned qualities back to him. If he doesn't really know that the rest of the members respect and care for him, he may even bolt. He may anyway. But his sense of belonging to and having a stake in the group should bring him back.

Again, the relationship is the tool for change. Only this time it's eight relationships, not one. In fact, one of the reasons to do therapy in a group setting is to provide a protected context in which members can aid and learn from one another. Here's a for-instance. One new fellow in group had significant unresolved issues with women. His mom had essentially abandoned him in his infancy, and he had been raised by the equivalent of a wicked step-mother.

Not too surprisingly, he ended up working in a female-dominated career, and experienced repeated conflicts with his women supervisors and co-workers. One of the other men in group, who also worked in a non-traditional field for men, had already resolved some similar issues with women.

In one session, the new man, embroiled once again in feelings of anger and helplessness, turned to the other fellow and asked, "How do you manage to work with those witches?" I'll never forget the reply, which was delivered with a wry smile, "I've had great success with being nice to them..."

This healing permission, coming from a fellow traveler who had negotiated the same path in struggling to overcome his blocks to happiness with self and others, carried a potency that could never have come from me. What a guy!

CHAPTER 4

Penis Envy

No psychological book would be complete without a mention of the notorious concept of Penis Envy. A lot of controversy surrounds this term. Most of us folks of the female persuasion, in fact, think it's a pretty hilarious idea. I have yet to encounter evidence of it in my practice, at least among the women ...

I had to rethink my position, though, when I took up mountain climbing. For the first time in my life, in my mid-thirties, I experienced penis envy. Severe penis envy. There we were, five hulking male specimens and I, high up on Mt. Rainier. The winds were fierce, the temperature daunting. And we were too many hours from base camp. One is supposed to get dehydrated while climbing, but I guess I wasn't, because I REALLY HAD TO GO. If you have a penis, going is pretty simple. But if your plumbing doesn't come with this feature, it ain't! You have to drop trou in whatever shred of privacy you can create above tree line, and bare ass to the unforgiving elements. If you haven't built enough character by climbing to that altitude, I guarantee this will do the trick.

I talked this over with my son Beaver, to get some male feedback, and he filled me in on another variety, Outboard Penis Envy. This form occurs mostly during the summer months, when the college crowd is boating for hours on end, fortified by many six packs of pop and whatever. I could see what he meant... The most severe attacks of penis envy, though, seem to be experienced by men who frequent locker rooms and stables.

Come to think of it, P.E. may have been behind some apparently irrational behavior in one of my groups. This is a women's group, understand, and it has a tendency to get a little outrageous from time to time. One of the members brought an athletic doll as an addition to the props. You know, the one whose parts are attached with velcro so that frustrated sports fans can vent their spleens by ripping him apart. He was well received, but someone made the observation that he wasn't a whole man... Sure enough, the next week another person showed up with a little detachable you-know-what. Don't blame me, it's not my fault! I even put the offending member away in a drawer, but they keep getting it back out and making the most obnoxious puns.

I'm not sure whether this qualifies as penis envy. I don't want to think about it too much. I do know one thing, though. He still doesn't have any balls.

CHAPTER 5

Couples

Couples are a special treat. Some of the best fun in my career has come from working with couples, straight and gay. And some of the greatest challenge. For one thing, most couples don't appear on my doorstep until the relationship is pretty much in shreds. Like two prizefighters in their opposite corners of the ring, each feeling powerless and cranky and not seeing many options. "We either duke it out or we stay in our respective corners with our arms crossed while Peg applies her therapeutic needle and thread to our tattered partnership."

If there was ever a time to call on Therapeutic Hope, this is it! At such moments, I remind myself that marriages are no longer forced on people by their parental units. So these two folks must have liked something about each other in the past, even if it's temporarily slipped their minds. Otherwise they wouldn't have gotten together.

Bearing this in mind, I find a way in the first meeting to interrupt the sparring and ask, "So how did you two get together in the first place? What the heck did you like about the other one, anyhow?" Then I watch their faces and bodies as they consider this question. At first, they are taken aback, probably because they weren't planning to come in and say flattering things about each other. Then they will usually smile a bit as they think back to their twitterpation. This is a good sign. Maybe there is hope. The sweet feelings are still in there somewhere. (If there was no twitterpation, or if they can't remember it, that's not so hopeful.)

47

I also listen to how they answer. Do they have tears in their eyes? Is there a romantic or nostalgic quality to their answer? Do they show respect or affection? Do they have to search and search to come up with a response? How do they look while listening to the positive things the other is offering? These responses are almost always quite sincere - will the partner let herself believe that?

Such non-verbal cues provide even more information about the nature of the relationship than does the content of the answers. And I need that information, because one of the things they are paying their dough for is the perspective of an impartial observer who can perceive things that escape them, and who knows what to do with that information.

What I do with it isn't too surprising. I offer it back to them as a present of hope, devoid of self- and other-badness. For example, he says to her, "You never listen to what I have to say!" She hears one more criticism, and begins to gird her loins for a defensive response. Having noticed the hurt look on his face, however, I may introject, "Did you hear how much he would like to be helpful to you?" "Huh?" "I think your partner would like very much to be appreciated and helpful, (I turn to him), is that right?" Nod. (I turn to her) "Do you understand" And so on. What we have here folks, is a failure to communicate!

Now I didn't just fall off the turnip truck. I know that this little interchange isn't going to save their relationship. What I'm aiming for is to disconcert. Shake them up a little, so that they start to question, even a teensy bit, the gloom and doom they have sunk into. Especially, I want to begin to ferret out the self- and other-badness that is woven through this partnership. The badnesses and unuseful script expectations that are influencing them without their knowing it.

I'm doing other stuff too. I'm modeling Paying Attention to the other. Because if she's doing a good job of that, she can't be listening to the antique beliefs and messages in her head. It's impossible to do both at once. And if she's tuned in to him instead of to the badness station, she will experience the whole interchange differently. Like she won't take what he's saying as a statement about her, but rather as one about him. Then she has a better chance of getting the real message, because she'll be having more of the relationship out in the air than in her head. Works better that way.

Something else. By paying close attention to him, her non-verbal communication is, "You're important to me. So is what you have to say." Now that's a powerful human message! And he gets it. I+ - Y+. It's hard for him to stay mad at her when she's genuinely paying him that kind of attention. He can do it, of course, but he has to really work at it.

Furthermore, I'm beginning to teach choice. That each of us has choice in how we interpret behavior. We can use our script frame of reference for interpretation, and then do the same old dances and feel the same old feelings, unhappy with self and others. Or we can stay in the present - in this world...- and have a wider range of possible feelings.

A word here about mending. Not everyone is in my office to salvage their relationships, And rightfully so, because sometimes changing the situation is necessary for problem-solving. The majority of couples, however, would prefer to continue the relationship if they had a glimmer of hope that they could enjoy it again. They just feel hopeless because they think they have Tried Everything. And now they can say, "We even tried marriage counseling!"

They generally haven't tried everything, however, because they were limited by their script options. So they may decide to give it another try, if they get a little glimmer of hope. I also have a bias. I have lots of them, in fact - every therapist does - but this one I reveal, so it's no secret. That bias is toward preserving relationships. These two people have put a lot of blood, sweat and tears into this relationship. Think of it as protecting an investment.

At the same time, part of what they are paying their dough for, in my opinion, is my help in their clarifying what they want, so that we are working to achieve their goals, not mine. What I tell them is this - I believe in the value of informed choices. It may be that if I can help them ferret the old business out of their partnership they will have new and important information about how they can get along. "Oh, I didn't know it could be like this...hmmm."

So if they haven't already decided to untie the knot, I may propose a trial period during which they can experiment with the new improved product, I+ - Y+ training of partners, and see how they like it. If they don't, they can return it with a money-back guarantee that they can still go their separate ways if that's what they want at that point. (The really sneaky part about doing it this way is that whether they decide to stay together or split, they'll probably go about either choice in a way that's kinder and gentler to each other and to themselves.)

Now practicing I+ - Y+ relating does not mean that there will be no conflict. In cases where the script decisions went something like, "The way to get along in this world is to always be nice," for instance, the couple may need to have more conflict. May need to learn the joys of "fair" fighting. See, unrelenting "niceness" tends to fester, and then the natural resentments that are part of any relationship are likely to leak out, to be expressed in hostile ways that the person didn't really intend, like guilt induction or jabs. Hostility is slippery, hard to handle, and preserves person-badness.

A good way to teach effective conflict is to use illustration. Here's an illustration of an illustration for you. Once upon a time I knew a couple who loved to fight. They had enormous respect for each other's skill with the gloves, and preferred this method of giving and getting strokes to any other. I learned a lot about the finer points of one-up-womanship and fun fighting from listening to tales of their exploits.

One of my favorites is his story of a shouting match spread over three days and seven different locations. (Degree of difficulty = 8.4) The climax followed a dramatic door-slamming, tire-squealing exit on his part. After spending the night with his brother, he returned home, lacing on his gloves, only to find her gone. She'd taken the kids and gone home to Mother. On the opposite coast. "I didn't mind the plane tickets for her and the kids so much," he said, his eyes shining with pride, "but she'd air freighted the dog!" Now there's a woman with some class!

Don't get me wrong here; I'm much more a dove than a hawk. I'm not trying to get couples to fight more, just better. Conflict is not a marker of failure in a relationship, it's simply the product of the fact that two people cannot possibly want, feel, or think exactly the same thing at the same time. They are not clones, so they differ. In fact, their differences are some of the reasons they were attracted to each other in the first place. If there's no sign of conflict, I start getting real curious. Are these folks individuals? Are they afraid to differ for some reason? What's the deal?

Couples can do conflict however they want. They can use it to Collect Evidence of someone's badness to support early script beliefs, for example, in which case they will feel awful. Or they can think of it as an opportunity for creative training, a raucous Flamenco with lots of castanets and stomping around. "I'm OK and so are you and you'd better listen up." Ole!

Individual style plays a big part here. I'm fond of banging and slamming while conflicting (it gives me time to search for the perfect retort, and also adds a nice dramatic touch). Husband Ragnar, however, being significantly bulkier and more imposing, gets excellent mileage out of the well placed scowl. It's entirely a matter of preference. Play around with it a bit until you develop your personal signature. A caution; don't get in too much of a rut - varying your routine keeps your audience alert and interested. TV sitcoms, friends, and novels provide stimulating source material.

My aim is to help folks move out of a victim position in which they are feeling bad because somebody done 'em wrong and into a self-assertive posture in which they are feeling pleased because they aren't letting that happen anymore. Anyone who is making sure that others treat him with respect is less cranky and nicer to be near.

To this end, I may have clients doing all sorts of unexpected and uppity stuff with each other in my office, all of which is aimed at interfering with their unquestioned frames of reference. And at having fun, so their kid part can't resist joining in. Substituting Getting the Other's Attention for guilt induction. Like what? Like having the little woman grab the big man by the lapels, stick her nose in his face, and say, "Listen up!" Or having one of them fall to the floor, roll over on his back, stick his paws in the air and cry, "I give."

Or standing on chairs, or giving the bronx cheer, or waving a hankie in surrender, or practicing parental finger-shaking (oh no, not the dreaded finger-shaking...). Folks begin to learn the difference between these two statements: "You really hurt me when you do that," vs., "Do that again, kiddo, and you're in deep ca-ca!" The first is guilt inducing, the second, designed to Get Your Attention. Get it? (A note here - I wouldn't, of course, use any physically provocative homework if there was the slightest chance of real or implied violence in the relationship.)

My red-headed friend Matilda used to leave signs in the kitchen for her teenagers,"Do the dishes or die." Clear, non-guilt inducing, potent and funny, so the kid part of them had a hard time not cooperating. It beats the heck out of, "I'll be disappointed in you if you don't do the dishes," because it teaches respect for law and order instead of total grievance recall.

Of course, she's also the one who would descend on her sons' unsuspecting grade school principal, bra-less and indignant, if she thought the kids needed her back-up for any reason. It's like this in adult relationships, too. The kid in each of us needs to know that we can count on that kind of support from our mate, and also that we'd better stay out of heck with them. One of the cartoons I have posted in my office shows one little boy telling another, "I've figured out a great new way to get along with my mom - she tells me what to do and I do it." ("The Family Circus," by Bil Keane)

These are the sorts of illustrations I use with couples. Helps them get the picture way easier than lengthy explanations on my part, learned as they may be. I'm playing with them as much as they'll let me, because this is the best way to teach them to play with each other. Which is the best way for them to train each other.

A few words about training. Remember, the aim of training significant others is to be happier with them, yourself, and the relationship. "Live in this world, and be satisfied..." This idea rubs some folks the wrong way. "Why should it be my job to make sure she treats me right? It's not fair. She should just do it without my having to ask or insist." Of course it's not fair. It's not unfair either. It's just life. Anyone who doesn't accept that isn't living in this world.

Even infants have to teach their parental units how to please them. And they do a darned good job of it too, since everyone in the vicinity knows clearly when they are pleased or displeased. Imagine a hungry new baby thinking to herself, "I'd sure like some milk about now, but it's not fair that I should have to cry for it, so I won't." She doesn't lie there feeling powerless and hurt about how people don't pay attention. No siree, it's "Gimme that milk right now!" (In resonating baby language, of course.)

Culturally, we've complicated this issue by supporting the idea that it's tacky to be clear about what we want. And a character flaw not to know, of course, what others want without their having to tell us. What a dopey idea. Just one more way to latch on to some badness feelings.

So I use more illustration. Like how I used to take Ragnar a cup of coffee in bed in the morning. But he usually wouldn't drink much of it and he never really thanked me. Then I could add another check to his badness list and even feel justified in having a 2.6 level sulk. He didn't appreciate my wifely helpfulness. And then if he wanted to, he could feel unjustly sulked at, and Gather Evidence about Women.

Finally, we got around to training each other about Morning Bed Coffee. (Probably because I exceeded the sulk limit once too often.) Turns out, he doesn't care much about Morning Bed Coffee one way or the other. It's me who adores it. In wanting to be loving and giving, I was doing for him what would have been just right for me. Meanwhile, guess who was going without MBC? Me. Because I hadn't asked for it. Now we've got it all straightened out - ask, and ye shall receive...

A story like this usually helps clients get over their training resistance. Especially when they see how much training raises the yummy level in a relationship. Because most folks do seem to enjoy pleasing their mates. "You're special, I'm special." It enhances one's immune system to say (or hear), "You're the most wonderful Ragnar in the Whole Wide World!"

If they show up at my door, most couples have been doing Backwards Training. Backwards training is getting your partner to do what you most detest or fear. Huh? Allow me to explain. Suppose that these two nice folks come into the office for the first time. Feeling some form of icky about their relationship. Pretty soon, we get around to what they Can't Stand about the other's behavior.

Like, "I can't stand it when she won't quit nagging me. She won't leave me alone!" And for her it might be, "I can't stand it when he withdraws and won't talk to me. I feel awful!" So I say to him, "Hmmm. What's the very best thing you can do to get her to nag you? I mean, if you really wanted her to bug you, how could you get her to do it?" "Huh? Why would I want to do that?" "Well, of course you don't want her to nag you, but if you did, I bet you know how you could get her to..."

Now she's sitting there knowing perfectly well how he gets her to do it - by withdrawing. So then I say to her, "And what's the thing you can do that's almost guaranteed to get him to withdraw?" Can you guess? That's right, nag. Unknowingly, each has gotten into the habit of doing the thing that's most likely to get them the response from the other that they hate. And probably experiencing that the other is making them do it. "What else can I do when she nags but withdraw?" "What else am I supposed to do when he won't talk to me?"

They may even know they are doing this dance but not seem to be able to stop. That's because the real motivation is out of their awareness. The real motivation is to Gather Evidence to substantiate early script beliefs about men, women, self, marriage, closeness, trust, and so on. To reinforce early decisions. Like, "Her nagging is one more proof that you can't get along with women." Or, "His withdrawal just shows how unlovable I am."

Time to get creative. I maintain that there are 9,002 different things he can do besides clam up in response to nagging. And if he wants to do something more fun and more powerful than Gathering Evidence, he can. (Author's aside here; since withdrawal is quite threatening to her inner little girl, and since it's one of his inner little boy's defenses, we don't have to consider all 9,002, just the ones that feature some form of giving, rather than withholding. They also have to be sincere, not hostile.)

Like what? Like sticking his tongue out with a twinkle in his eye and a naughty grin on his face. Or crawling across the floor on his hands and knees, kissing her feet and begging forgiveness. Or starting a squirt gun fight. Or putting his hands gently on her shoulders, looking her squarely in the eye, and telling her that she's right about what she's saying and he'll mend his ways. (And then doing it)

The truth is, any new response that's from an I'm OK - You're OK position will change the dance. It's hard for her to keep doing the same steps if her partner switches tempo. She may get thrown off her stride and start following his lead. Even in the unlikely event that she keeps nagging, if he's doing something like the above instead of withdrawing, he's changed the 50% that he's contributing to the relating, so the dance looks real different. And feels better, since he'd have a very hard time thinking Bad Thoughts about her while mischievously sticking out his tongue. Right at that very moment, he likes her. And himself.

One couple I saw in the olden days got the hang of this training business real well. First, understand that many, maybe most, folks in couple's counseling have the secret agenda that I will change the other one so that they can live happily ever after. Pretty understandable. Anyhow, one day this neat couple came in. The very nice woman was at her wit's end with her very likeable husband who'd been acting like a stinker, to make a long story short.

I'm pretty sure both of them expected me to roll up my sleeves and join in the effort to Improve him. Nope. I did tell him that lots of folks act stinkery to preserve self-badness. And that stinkeriness was also a good way to get other people (like wives) on their cases, so they could pay attention to what a critical wife they had instead of getting on their own cases for their stinkeriness. So he could think about that.

But then I asked her whether she would stay married to him if he never changed an ounce. After some uncomfortable thought, she allowed as how she would. "OK, since you've decided to stay with him," I said, "it's your job to make him treat you the way you want him to."

That didn't sit too well with her at first, but after some training in unreasonableness and uppitiness, she took on the task. And was a very fast learner. The next week when they came in for their "Peg Appointment," she was beaming and he was looking quite relieved. It seems that he had spent some of the rent money on a rather expensive pair of new shoes for himself. Very stinky behavior.

In the past, she would have felt angry, powerless, and Disappointed in him, and he would have felt guilty and resentful. Pretty unpleasant for both of them. This time, however, she changed the dance. "I made him give them to me," she announced triumphantly, (he's huge and she's tiny, by the way) "and I haven't decided what I'll do with them yet, but I may give them to the Salvation Army. I may even throw them in the garbage!"

Outrageous! She moved out of her script and into happiness with self and others. In this case she took the lead in changing the dance, but it could just as well have been him, since they were both sincere and motivated folks who loved each other. Beats me how she made him give them to her, but I don't care. The point is that she gave herself permission to rock and roll, and no longer had any reason to be mad at him. And he couldn't sustain his self-badness.

Once a couple has turned over a new record like this, we can easily do some archeology if necessary. Like what was true in his childhood that he grew up feeling so bad about himself and getting people to punish him? And how come it made sense for her to grow up not trusting men and not knowing how to assert herself on her own behalf? The repeated stuck places in a relationship are almost always metaphors for dilemmas each person had to deal with as a kid.

(Note: if anyone is worried about the welfare of the shoes here, they don't Get It.)

See why working with couples is so exciting? And why I think people are downright amazing? That's not to say that I don't have the occasional couple session that I'd like to charge double for. Usually, that's because they won't hardly stop fighting long enough for me to get a word in edgewise. So I get less and less reasonable. I might say, "Do you two really want to pay dough for doing here what you can do at home for free?"

Or I might get up and go to the bathroom. Or if they seem locked into Who's To Blame, I might go to the board, write down each of their names, and start keeping score to see who's getting ahead. "You really scored with that one, Abner." "Outstanding rejoinder, Murgatroid!"

Again, the aim is to disconcert. As therapist, I need to have a certain number of behavior samples from them in order to know what to do. But after a while, their fighting from the same old positions is just a waste of time, so I interrupt, perhaps in an outrageous way, so we can get on with getting happy with self and others. Since 99.99% of the folks I work for are sincerely motivated, they get themselves unstuck pretty quick in response to my rude interruption, and get back on track. Hooray!

Then there's the .01%. Any couple (or client) can be much better at not getting happy than I am at Making Them Happy. One such couple came in a few times and remained impervious to any of my hopeful and earnest interventions. Then they didn't show up for a session and fell off the earth. In response to my requests for dough, I eventually received a note which said, in effect, that I hadn't done them any good, so they weren't paying for the session they didn't cancel.

After all my hard work! Afire with righteous indignation, I drafted a witty and scathing response in which I informed them that I had found people's progress in therapy to be highly correlated with whether or not they paid any attention to what I said. Then I tore it up and enjoyed the rest of my day. I didn't care to dance any more to that tune.

Now, I know that these folks had childhoods, too, and I understand some of the reasons for their behavior. I even have empathy for them. That doesn't mean I have to like being treated that way. Of course, it's my script issue that I hate it when people are so rude as to not let me help them. The nerve! Ah, the vicissitudes of life in Therapy Land...

Couples can also renew one's faith in humankind. Once a man came in because he was having anxiety attacks. After a few sessions of Getting to Know Each Other, he revealed that he had been engaging in physical fights with his wife regularly for a number of years. She would needle him and he would respond by hitting. I said, "You'll have to stop that. And not for the reasons you think. You'll have to stop because it's too scary for you to be out of control like that and to be such a bad guy in everyone's eyes."

He acted as if an enormous burden had been lifted off his shoulders. He had permission to stop collecting self-badness, and start taking some control. Permission to act like a decent human being. To my knowledge, he has not resumed the physical abuse, and no longer attacks himself with anxiety. They did lots of individual and couple's therapy and were still together at last report.

I want to be clear about one thing. This was a dance they did together, and each changed so that they could do a happier one. In no way, however, does her part in the dance excuse him from responsibility for hitting her. No matter how obnoxious she may have acted, he still had other options - she did not and could not make him hit her. Their couple's myth had been that she made him lose control. By telling him to stop, I acted from the belief that he did, in fact, choose whether to have control or not, and that he was not evil. He just thought he was.

Don't assume that these folks typify abusive relationships. They may or they may not. Just note that they are great examples of how people who are stuck in their scripts can change their life courses and give up people-badness. Pretty darned impressive.

CHAPTER 6

Diagnosis

A controversial subject. Therapy School publishes a great Big Green Book on diagnosis, and every therapist should read it, keep a copy on her bookshelf, and know when to use it.(1) And when not to. I like to use Pat the Psychiatrist's favorite diagnosis most of the time - "Human Being." (Don't look for it in the BGB, although they do have a category [V71.09] for absence of a disorder...) I find Pat's diagnosis the most useful, even though many of my clients who don't think they deserve a place in the human race resist it rather vigorously for awhile. I assure them, however, that I have been to Therapy School, and that they have to trust me on that particular diagnosis. It's for their own good....

Of course, what I'm trying to stay away from, here, are any more ways for the client to think badly of himself, in this case by applying to himself a label which is likely to engender feelings of inadequacy. I include in this category newer, popular labels like "codependent". I really like Dr. McDermott's statement, "People aren't 'dysfunctional' - they're just human." (25, p.12)

To get some perspective, let's take a look at what psychodiagnosis is good for. It's useful if it accurately describes something that is clearly different from something else, and then tells us what to do about it. Diagnosis may also be useful if it tells us there is nothing we can do about the condition it describes.

Trouble is, some of the time diagnosticians disagree about what is clearly different from something else, and about who falls into which categories. Further, having a label for someone's condition, even if accurate, may not tell us what to do. So for the clinician, knowing when not to diagnose often means knowing when that approach won't be useful in treatment.

So, just to contradict myself, I'll say that the therapist needs to make an initial assessment of whether to "diagnose" in the traditional sense, or not. And she needs to have enough psychology under her belt that she knows how to do that. The tricky thing about diagnosis is that, unless you're using "Human Being" (for both of you), it's easy for the therapist and client to slip into Big-Person, Little-Person positions relative to each other. One of us has a Diagnosis and one of us doesn't...

Since this is so easy to fall into anyway, I'll do whatever I can think of to stay out of it. To do so, I tend to use diagnostic terms you won't find in the Big Green Book. Besides Human Being, these include Too Fussy, Too Scandinavian, (being Scandinavious, I can use this one), Too Helpful, Too Worried, Too Careful, and so on. These are easily understood and harder to feel bad about. They can sort of be viewed as virtues that have gotten a bit out of hand. They can also apply to most anyone, no matter which side of the couch she's on.

Another sort of diagnosis I use is script diagnosis. That simply means being tuned into the client, Getting to Know him and the world he lives in. Getting to know his beliefs about self, others, and life, especially those early decisions which are interfering with living in this world, being satisfied, and happy with self and others. The client and I do this diagnosing together.

There are times when someone with a practice like mine needs to do more traditional diagnosis, however. Generally, those times are when talking together isn't all that's necessary to help the client achieve happiness and satisfaction in his life. At these times, I need to make an outside referral.

Like with substance abuse. I don't believe that psychotherapy is effective as a means to get addicted people to stop drinking or using. So I may refer a client to an alcohol or drug care program for assessment or treatment, knowing that therapy will be useless until he or she stops abusing. I'm delighted at the increased education and awareness about drug and alcohol abuse, because it's resulting in more folks getting clean and sober, so they can be in charge of their lives.

So that's one situation in which I may refer out. The most frequent type of referral I make, however, is medical. Again, these referrals are made when I suspect that talking alone won't achieve what the client wants. Sometimes this is because I suspect a medical condition, like thyroid imbalance or neurological problems, but most often it's for depression.

The big "D." One of the most common things that ails us. Not to be considered a character flaw, even though it often is, by observers, and especially by the depressee. Creeping self-badness again. Also one of the most commonly missed. According to a recent study reported by Ron Winslow in the Wall Street Journal, family practice docs may miss it half of the time or more.(Fall, 1988)

Which is a shame, because it is usually an easy ailment to treat. If you don't have Antidepressantaphobia, that is. Antidepressantaphobia seems about as common as depression, unfortunately, in the general public, and even among some health professionals. Its symptoms include fear of taking medication for depression, and severe reluctance to get informed about the subject. "A don't confuse me with facts" position.

Treatment of antidepressantaphobia is simple. First, there has to be a contract that the phobic person would like to move from a phobic position to an informed one. From an informed position, the person can then make a factually-based decision about the advisability of a trial of medication, rather than have a knee-jerk reaction. An informed judgement, rather than a prejudiced one.

Once the contract is established, then the next step is fact-gathering. I consider a visit to a good psychiatrist to be a sensible way to start gathering facts. There is so much new research data in the field that it's difficult for anyone to keep up with. Since keeping up is their business, these folks will have saved you the trouble of going to medical school yourself, or of trying to sort through all that info on your computer net or at your local library.

If you want to, of course, you can still do that. Any therapist can refer you to some good reading material on depression and its treatment. You can judge for yourself. I have a number of handouts of this nature that l give clients. You will find, if you look into it, that the majority opinion is that the most effective treatment for depression is a combination of talk therapy and medication, not either one alone.

I agree, from my own experience on both sides of the couch. Throughout the time that I've been in practice, I've been fortunate enough to have excellent psychiatric support, and to have worked with a broad range of client-folks, including those with serious psychiatric disabilities. Over the years, I've cured myself of Psychiatricmedicationaphobia (Psychiatricmedicationaprejudice?)

Some conditions won't get better just because you talk at them. Diabetes is an example. Modification of life-style may help, but sometimes not enough. Medication (insulin, in this case) may be needed to prolong life and to improve the quality of life of the diabetic person. Same with depression. As with diabetes, something is bio-chemically out of whack in a person who is depressed. There are lots of different ways in which he or she may be out of whack, and all degrees of severity of out of whackness.

A few folks get depressed enough that they become psychotic or kill themselves. Most, however, just get grimmer and tireder and crankier and tenser and tearier and more hopeless and slowed way down and can't sleep. They even may lose their interest in sex. All these are physical symptoms caused by the out of whackness, and indicative of depression. They are not caused by and do not indicate lack of character. Folks who are out of whack in this way usually attribute these symptoms to character flaws, however, and want to deal with them by gritting their teeth and toughing it out.

That makes no more sense to me than does trying to deal with diabetes by gritting of teeth and toughing it out. So I talk with folks like this about options. I give them some information about depression - what it means, what it doesn't mean, what can be done about it. Depending on what I know about their life style and beliefs, this info may be about exercise, nutrition, or electric light therapy, as well as about talk therapy and medical therapy. Antidepressants.

My aim is to promote thinking. The majority of clients that I have talked to about depression and meds have similar responses at first. Their prejudicial part may have Very Strong Opinions that anti-depressant medications are for the weak, those who do things the Easy Way. That proper Working Through of a depression necessarily involves quite a lot of pain and suffering, or else it's cheating.

And their kid part, understandably, is scared. Scared of the unknown, mostly. "If I put this substance into my body, what might happen? I'm afraid I won't have control anymore. What if it's addicting, in spite of what the docs say? Will I like it so much I don't want to stop? What if it doesn't help anyway? Maybe it gives you an artificial feeling. How do I know I'm not copping out? What will my friends think?"

On the assumption that the client can think as well as I can, I urge gathering of information. Data and facts, not evidence. I often recommend a medical consultation with a psychiatrist as part of that process. I also may share my own experiences with taking antidepressant medication. Recurrent depressions seem to run in my family, and I have used five different antidepressants at various times over the last 16 years. Each has been helpful.

Clients have appreciated my being willing to do this. "Oh, you mean regular, well adjusted, people like shrinks get depressed? And even take meds? And even aren't embarrassed by it? Hmmm." My aim is to demystify and normalize this option, so folks deal with the question from their reality-testing part, not their scared and defensive parts. It's not a good idea to have a kid in charge of making one's medical decisions.

Over the time I've been in practice, I've seen clients profit immensely from antidepressant medications. One comment was particularly striking, "I feel like I've joined the human race!" I can relate to that - I've always been able to function while depressed, but boy, was I grim. I compare it to hiking up a mountain with or without a 40-pound backpack. I can do it either way, but what a difference that weight makes...

I view doing talk therapy while depressed in the same way. You can do it either with or without meds, but if the meds are effective, you can do it more efficiently and enjoy the scenery along the way. Have a more pleasant journey.

Meds don't solve everything. They all have some side effects, which can present dif-fic-ulties, minor or major, depending on the medication and on the person. If they relieve the symptoms of the depression, which they usually do, in my experience, all that happens is that the person is back in whack chemically.

In other words, can now sleep normally, has his usual energy level, isn't irritable, doesn't cry for no apparent reason, feels optimistic, has his regular sex drive, and so on. With his usual faculties at his disposal, he can address his therapeutic tasks with energy and optimism. The depression isn't cured by the meds. It is relieved.

There's exciting medical news these days from the halls of Therapy School. The more they discover about brain chemistry, the more ways we have to help people. Some of the newer antidepressants are also proving useful in the treatment of chronic pain, obsessive-compulsive disorders, anxiety disorders, and some eating disorders. Far out - I'm glad to have more options for helping folks become more satisfied and happy with self, others, and life.

One caution: In conjunction with antidepressant use, a number of clients have reported sudden, unexplained urges to laugh. This effect could have widespread ramifications and is being closely studied.

CHAPTER 7

Home Offices

There's no place like home. There's especially no place like home as a setting for therapeutic endeavor. Where else could one hear the patter of little feet? No, not kids. Mice, scurrying happily across the attic floor above us as we had evening group meetings. Once again, Therapy School never said what to do about that. Oh well....

They never told me I could excuse myself from group to participate in a family row either, but I did once. I had a capable co-leader, so the group was in good hands, but it's still a highly unusual therapist maneuver. I'm certainly not recommending it, mind you, but it didn't seem to impede anyone's therapeutic progress. Therapist as human being.

Like many therapersons who practice at home, I decided to do so for financial reasons. Ragnar was in school full time, and dough was tight, so it made sense to reduce overhead. I didn't expect mice to be part of my new overhead....

I gave myself a fair bit of Fear and Trembling over the move home. Would my clients think I wasn't a Real Therapist if I weren't surrounded by an official office with a number on the door? Bravely, I hung my Diplomas and Certificates of Realness in plain sight, and forged ahead.

This little vignette illustrates the concept of projection quite well, so I'll seize this opportunity to get psychological for a moment. As you might have predicted, only three people ever questioned my realness - me, myself, and I. I was projecting my own lack of acceptance of myself out onto my current and prospective clients and expecting them to view me that way. A little time on the client side of the couch cleared that up.

Somewhat to my surprise, I loved practicing at home. I guess I could have predicted that, since I've been to Therapy School and recognize how much a comfortable, relaxed setting contributes to Getting to Know someone. This was a comfy home, so the therapy was comfy. At that time, we were lucky enough to be living in a sweet little old farmhouse which had a lovely paneled study with an outside entrance. The house had been sitting there for about 50 years, growing its apple orchard and its plum and pear trees just for our enjoyment. Merely driving in the driveway would lower a person's blood pressure five points.

Pretty therapeutic, huh? Even though the surrounding countryside was being gobbled up by suburbs and shopping centers, our acre and a half created a peaceful little oasis. Clients unanimously adored it and were cranky when I moved to a regular office after five years there. I was a bit cranky myself, but it was time.

Home practice isn't for everyone, though, because of the transparency involved. No client who enters your home can maintain the fiction that you live under the couch in your office. Here you are in your real live house with your real live family and your real live pets. Exposed. Clients know how you decorate, what kind of cars you drive, what sort of housekeeper you are, and maybe even what you're having for dinner.

They inevitably learn some of how you interact with Ragnar, and how Wally and Beaver are getting along this week. They may even develop relationships of their own with Wally and Beaver. "Hi, Beav, nice job you're doing on the lawn." "Thanks." Wally was kind enough to change someone's flat tire once. That's not taught in Therapy School.

As you can imagine, all this is going to influence the nature of the therapeutic relationship considerably. It's going to be full of who you are, as well as who the client is. The Getting to Know and the Nosiness are more reciprocal, maybe more fair. The way I look at it, this balance promotes more equality in the partnership and mitigates against a Big Person - Little Person set up.

There are other ways to view it, too, but this is how I prefer to think about it. I'm aware that my comfort with being so Known has its narcissistic elements. I don't have to scare myself with that by making it into badness. No matter what my office setting, my clients sense the "show-off" part of my personality, as they will be aware of the personality parts of any therapist they hire. Whether we therapersons like to admit this or not, it's true.

How I accept the less adorable parts of me is much more important to clients than what the less adorable parts are. OK, so I'm sometimes corny, or obnoxiously pleased with myself, or even rude. Or I may accidentally hurt someone's feelings. That's a true part of who I are, too, along with the more swell things I are.

What you see is what you get. Like I said, this is a real relationship, too, as real and valid as any other either of us is having at the time. Not perfect, but Good Enough. So I assume at the outset that there will be times when we will disappoint one another and ourselves. To try to avoid that would require avoiding the commitment of the relationship. Never being willing to risk another dance. How sad.

Part of what the client is paying his dough for is the modeling that I do when one of us blunders. How I handle his checks to me that bounce, or his revelations of self-badness. And how I deal with my calling him by someone else's name, or getting his appointment time mixed up. Not only must I model taking appropriate responsibility for my screw-ups, even though they are unintentional, but I must also show him by my actions how not to wallow in guilt or self-flagellation.

The only way to teach happiness with self and others is to live it. What's the term - walk what you talk? Practicing in your home is a special way to do this. In Therapy School, they don't tell you what to do when your Puppy jumps up on your client and runs her nylons. Well, what you do is, you pay for a new pair, express your regret, and make it clear that part of what she gets in dealing with you is Puppy. Part of who you are as therapist is the fact that you practice in your home and include Puppy (and Kitty) in your life, as well as her. And that that's OK.

Clients don't need the responsibility of thinking they are your reason for living. When you practice at home, they can clearly see that they are not - that your life is full of family and pets and soccer and holidays. And that your piano is usually dusty and that you have dandelions. Big Person illusions can't survive under such revealing conditions.

I also think there is something rather gracious about inviting clients to have their relationship with me in my home. Here's this special room for them in my house. How nice. Home practice models a hospitable sort of openness and comfort with being known about. And a lack of hypocrisy. When I'm working with them on throwing off the bonds of perfectionism, they know I mean it, because they've seen the piles of paper on the floor and the windows that need to be washed. And they know that in spite of such sins, I fully expect to get into heaven.

Also, it's my opinion that all psychotherapy would be better if it included pets. Of course, I think almost anything is better if you add pets, so I'm biased. I even used to be a dog trainer of sorts in one of my former lives. I've been heard to tell an occasional client to "sit" and "stay", in fact. (They were appropriate interventions at the time - you'll have to trust me on that...)

It not just bias, though. Some studies evidently have found that stroking kitties lowers one's blood pressure. There are other therapeutic considerations as well - Kitty and Puppy are great models when it comes to demanding and appreciating strokes, a fact which I point out to clients. I also point out how appealing that kind of hedonism is. And that purring and wagging when you are getting what you asked for from someone is a very smart way of increasing your chances of getting more of it. So they can learn from Puppy and Kitty how to stroke and purr and wag with their friends and mates and live more happily ever after. Purring and self-badness are mutually exclusive.

The kid part of virtually everyone either had pets or wished they did. So having Puppy cavorting around helps that kid part trust that I'm OK, even if I am a grown-up. And that kid part gets to watch how I interact with Puppy when Puppy does his 75-pound-lap-dog number at me. Ooof! Remember, it's that smart kid part of the client that made those early decisions about life, and you'd better believe that any shrink is being checked out from that perspective.

It only makes sense that a kid is going to like me better if I don't get all worked up when Kitty uses my couch for a scratching post. My position is that kitties are more important than furniture, and that's hard for a kid to resist. Further, I'm not fussy about hairs. More often than not, a client who's been sitting in my office at home for a while will leave wearing the dog on her skirt. I figure that's why nature made lint rollers, and I offer her the one I keep by the door.

If the parental part of a client gets fussy about hair generosity, I may even tell one of my favorite Wally and Beaver stories to calm her down. One morning all four of us were having breakfast in the kitchen. Ragnar, Beaver, and I were at the table and Wally was getting some milk out of the fridge, when he paused and looked critically at Beaver's navy blue velour robe. It was covered with evidence of Kitty, since Beav is her favorite human. "How come I have to have a plain old bathrobe," says Wally, "when Beaver gets a fur one?"

A real drawback to the swell waterfront office that I have now is that I can't have pets there. Well, I could, but it would take Kitty all day to get over her snit about the cat carrier and the ferry ride and it wouldn't be worth the trouble. At least I don't have to keep a lint roller there, since my clients don't get furry.

CHAPTER 8

Boundaries

Some boundary considerations. That's the main deal about a home office - the boundaries differ. Boundaries are the protective limits surrounding the therapeutic relationship that keep it on track. The therapeutic contract is one of them. It's a clearly specified statement of what the client is in therapy to change about his life. Whatever he needs to do in order to live more in this world, and be satisfied... Like "I'm here to learn how to hold a job and then do it." Or "My contract is to finish my divorce and get on with my life."

Contracts for change will be the same in any setting. But what about the relationship contract? That's not so clearly specified, and each person's picture of it is different; influenced by all the personal and cultural expectations discussed earlier.

If we wrote it out, a therapeutic relationship agreement might look like this: You and I agree to meet regularly for the purpose of effecting the changes you want in your life. You will pay me x amount of dough per hour in payment for my using my experience, intelligence, and therapeutic skill to aid you in your efforts. I will provide the setting for our meetings and will show up ready to work at the specified times. You will also show up motivated and ready to engage in therapeutic nosiness and problem solving.

I agree to operate in a professional, ethical, and legal manner, which includes keeping what we do in confidence. You agree to participate

in good faith, doing your darndest to achieve your goals. You take
responsibility for solving your own problem, using me as a tool. I'll
be responsible for knowing lots of ways to go about that, but not for
working any harder than you are, or for being any smarter than you
are.

My responsibilities include not taking advantage of you, and seeing
that you don't do so with me. It's my job to make sure that the fee
we agree on is satisfactory to me, and your job to do the same for
yourself. This is not a caretaking relationship, in either direction,
but a reciprocal one.

We will develop feelings for one another, but that is not part of the
contract. It's just what people do when they Get to Know one
another. So we will have respect for and trust in one another, and
high regard, and likely some cross feelings too, from time to time.
We will talk about and use all of these feelings, in the service of
achieving your therapeutic goals.

We'll be intimate, but we won't become part of each other's social
circles - that's outside the bounds of the relationship contract. Our
focus is goal-directed, and multiple levels of relating are apt to
confuse and detract from that focus. We couldn't be that emotionally
intimate if you thought I might show up at your dinner table, or at
your job, or join your crowd while you were out dancing.

If I appeared in your life without my therapist hat on, you'd probably
feel spied on. Like I didn't belong in this part of your life. Which
I don't. And, as my client, you don't belong in that part of my life
either, however much I may enjoy you. You can probably see where
this is leading. If my office is in my home, you, as client, are in some
sense both exposed to and included in my private life.

Maybe you'd rather not know that my windows are dirty. Maybe I'd
prefer that you didn't know what I was having for dinner. But you
do know this stuff. So we have the job of staying focused on the

therapeutic task at hand, even though our relationship in a sense is broader than some therapy partnerships. You have to be comfortable with a therapist who's a known quantity - a fallible human with dust on her piano. I have to be comfortable with being visible. I have to assume that it's useful for clients to see how "regular" I am, and how comfortable I am with that.

Obviously, this sort of transparency will work for some therapists and some clients, and not for all. That's cool. Some clients would be thrown by looking out of the window and seeing Ragnar running in circles on the lawn carrying a canoe on his head, for instance. (He was only practicing for the next canoe and portage race...) For that matter, some therapists wouldn't want to go public with a husband like that. I happen to think he's very cute when he's being herky.

Of course, no office space is immune from intrusions across the supposedly pristine boundaries of therapeutic privacy. My "regular" office opens onto a park. We can gaze out over the grass at the magnificent Olympic mountains, as ferries toodle back and forth in front of us on sparkling Puget Sound. Does that sound too good to be true, too therapeutic for words?

Well, it almost is. And we also have, free of charge, a goose who comes to the window at the most dramatic moments, tilts her head curiously as she looks in at whoever is in tears at the moment, and says "HONK". And little kids who throw stuff at the glass doors and rattle them, trying to get in. And a train that goes by at regular intervals, huffing and tooting, on the other side of the building. Some of those engineers are real virtuosos on the whistle, let me tell you.

And in the summer, we often hold group in competition with the spirited volleyball game outside the door. Thump! Crash! Cheer! Curse! And the noise from the volleyball players outside is even worse...

My office windows are silvered for privacy. That's supposed to help, but it turns into a drawback instead when a nubile young bikini-clad maiden decides to use one of them for a mirror. Talk about distractions. What's a therapist to do? They never told me in Therapy School... When the train hoots I usually just say that there's no extra charge for the entertainment.

When I worked in Beautiful Downtown Bellevue I had an even more intrusive experience. A religious looking sort of fellow walked into my waiting room, opened the door to my group room, which had a sign on it reading, "In session, please wait," and strolled right on in. He stood there in his robe trying to sell us flowers even as I said, "You can't come in here." I had to get up and back him all the way out into the hall. He never did stop trying to make a sale. Now that guy didn't respect boundaries....

And you know what? People still cure themselves of their distresses and dif-fic-ulties just fine, even with all the commotion. Aren't humans amazing? The therapy adventure may hardly resemble the nice, neat ivory tower sort of experience outlined in T.S., and it still works.

It took me a while to have coffidence in this, though, partly because I formed the impression in Therapy School that therapeutic relationship boundaries are sort of like the Ten Commandments, sacred in themselves, revealed on the Mount, and cast in stone. And that something unspeakably awful will happen if they are not preserved as taught. Real life, though, is not that neat. However respectful I am of my client's right to privacy, I may still run into her, literally, on the soccer field. Women's soccer is a big deal in my area.

The Book of Therapy doesn't cover encounters of the soccer kind. I sort of figured, though, that if something like this happened between me and one of my clients, that I might have to turn in my helper badge, or at least understand that the trust in the relationship was severely impaired, and we'd have to spend lots of time and dough repairing it.

I haven't found that to be true. When something like this occurs, I ask the person in session what it was like for her to encounter me in this fashion, and we talk about any discomfort she may have had. I also humorously apologize for showing up in her outside life like that, even though we both know it was an accident, as a way of letting her know that I know it probably felt intrusive to her. Especially if I knocked her down - can't allow a score, after all, any soccer player knows that.

I believe most therapeutic relationships can handle, usually can even profit from, reminders that we are two humans who have become important to each other. Take the question of Presents. Presents, either way, are supposed to be a "no, no." The client who brings a gift probably has Issues around needing to please, or some such, so the gift must be refused, and the Issues thoroughly analyzed.

The therapist who gives a present no doubt has dangerous counter-transference Issues and must immediately report for supervision and treatment. Most of the time, all this seems kind of silly to me. Like we must examine every move either of us makes in case it contains some unrecognized badness. Well, gee, this is exactly what I'm trying to teach folks to do less of in the rest of their lives. My believability quotient would go way down if I was saying one thing and doing another, and then where would we be?

One of my clients brought in a string of Christmas tree bubble lights one year, because we'd been talking about Christmases past and how we both missed these old fashioned tree lights. Soon after that, she had been delighted to come across bubble lights in a store and bought us each some. I was ready to pay her for mine when she said "All this therapist-client stuff aside, I want to make a gift of them to you. My treat." I think it would have been insulting and Big-persony of me to argue, so I didn't. I thanked her.

Other clients have given me lovely photographs they have taken, books they have particularly enjoyed, ornaments they have made, flowers, and so on. I figure the only reasonable thing to do is to treasure them. If you want to get real psychological about it, maybe the client wants to leave a part of himself with me. That's usually OK with me. If bringing presents or doing things for me seem to present a pattern that is relevant to their script, I'll bring it up at some time in context, and we'll see what emerges.

In the therapist-client relationship, the emphasis is so much on what the therapist is giving, that, even though the relationship is really reciprocal, it can seem kind of one-sided. So I think it's often a good idea to share other giving in this way. It feels yummy.

I have also given gifts to clients for celebrations like births and weddings. Such presents usually take the form of cards or champagne toasts, but I have trouble resisting baby clothes and stuffed bunnies, and so I usually don't. I have even gone to some client weddings, hospital rooms, and funerals. I don't believe I've impeded anyone's therapeutic progress by doing so.

Keep in mind here that, even with folks who have very serious problems - physical, emotional, whatever - my goal is still to help them Live in this World, and be Satisfied, and Happy with Self and Others. Pat the Psychiatrist has been known to say, "Do what's in the books as long as it works, and when it doesn't work, do what does." So boundaries are important things to be aware of, but remember that the ones surrounding the therapeutic relationship exist to serve the above goal.

Most of the folks I work with have pretty good boundaries already - their early training taught them to notice that there are other humans in the world who differ from them and who have to be taken into account and respected. On the other hand, a few clients have been pretty intrusive, like the brother of a new client who harassed me for a date, or the client who threatened me with bodily harm. In cases like these, I call for reinforcements, even if that seems to violate the relationship boundaries.

And I've called the cops, too, when I believed a client to be suicide-bound. That's about all I can do when the therapeutic alliance and his other resources don't appear to be strong enough to support the person's willingness to keep living and problem solving.

That situation is rare, however. Even when a person is depressed and feeling hopeless, somewhere inside them is a scrappy part that wants to live and feel better. So I'll do darned near anything I can to connect with that part. Cajole, challenge, persuade, act bored, tease, yell, stand on my head, whatever I think might work. I'm aiming for a decision, from the client, once and for all, to live. It's very hard to help someone learn to be happy in the world if they're dead.

You see, some folks decided as youngsters that the only way to get along in their situation was to be dead. I know, that sounds screwy, but some circumstances are so crazy or punitive that such a conclusion makes a kind of sense. Especially to a kid. So he writes a script for himself that ends self-destructively. He might be aware of having done so, or he might not.

Here's an example of how someone could decide they should be dead. One of my group clients did not value himself and appeared to be headed for self-destruction. One of the things I knew about his background was that his mom had experienced some psychotic episodes when he was growing up.

In group one evening, he remembered an early scene in which he was playing noisily in the living room. Mom was harried. "Shut up," she yelled, "you're driving me crazy!" "Did you do that?" I asked softly. "Yes!" He sobbed as he relived the scene and felt the awful feelings he had as a little boy. He had grown up believing on some level that he was responsible for her psychotic episodes, and therefore didn't deserve to live.

Well, we got that grandiose idea straightened out in a hurry, and he decided that maybe he wasn't such a bad sort after all, and was going to live and enjoy himself, even if Mom was crazy or unhappy. Aren't people awesome!

If I think a client is headed toward killing himself or getting someone else to kill him, I'll go for a "No-suicide" contract. The wording Bob and Mary Goulding teach is this - "I won't kill myself, accidentally or on purpose, no matter what."(11) That about covers contingencies, doesn't it? Whatever the client may think, we really can't get anywhere on the task of accomplishing what he came in for until he closes this trap door.

Closing and locking the suicide trap door generally takes two separate decisions. One is from the adult part of the client. That is, he decides to live at first because that makes sense, and because he has some sort of faith that his life will get better. The second decision is from his kid part and usually comes later in therapy, at a point where he GETS IT that life can be terrific! Then he's solidly there.

Occasionally, a client makes both shifts at once. Like the person in one of my groups who was being heavily challenged by all of the rest of us on his self-destructive path. Finally, he let go of the last of his defenses against this caring pushiness and said "I won't kill myself, accidentally or on purpose, no matter what." But he didn't sound really solid with it. Someone asked to hear it again. Just as he was repeating the statement, the train went by. He was drowned out. "WHAT?" I yelled, "I CAN'T HEAR YOU." "I WON'T KILL MYSELF, ACCIDENTALLY OR ON PURPOSE, NO MATTER WHAT," he shouted at the top of his voice. None of us entertained the slightest doubt at that point, I can assure you....

CHAPTER 9

Being Too Psychological

Can we talk? OK, what does "being Too Psychological" really mean? First of all, it means that Everything anyone does or says has to have an Important Psychological Meaning, preferably unconscious. And that if we don't examine everything for that hidden meaning, we aren't doing our jobs and could lose our helper badges. Sounds like a lot of work to me.

I've noticed that lots of the time when I'm being thoroughly and obediently psychological, I'm forgetting to use common sense. One of Eric Berne's contributions to Therapy School was that he encouraged therapists to look at interactions and other behavior the way a kid would - simply. You know, like "the emperor's new clothes?" Pat the Psychiatrist calls it "telling the simple truth."

Works good. Have a look at the real person sitting here, rather than at the labels put on her by herself and by others. Now I know why some teachers don't want to read last year's reports on the kids in their new class. At least, not until they've had their own look at the kids.

Some clients get kind of put out with me at first if they've gone to the trouble to figure out the labels for things and I'm not necessarily too interested. Like, "She verbally abused me." Huh? What did she actually do - yell, lie, call you names, swear, threaten bodily harm, scream, say she was going to leave you - what? The behavioral information is useful, the label isn't, except to Gather Evidence. So another way to be Too Psychological is to speak in abstract terms a lot, rather than specific behavioral ones.

The most serious cases of this that I've encountered have occurred when both partners in a relationship were shrinks. In my opinion, extreme caution should be exercised by anyone considering such a pairing, since psychologicalness can easily reach critical mass and explode, scattering radioactive bits of nomenclature throughout the neighborhood, and rendering it virtually uninhabitable until decontaminated.

Another common way to be Too Psychological is to be oblivious to your context. There's a time and place. For instance, a friend of mine was walking in Stanley Park, BC, with his wife. They were enjoying the lovely setting and hadn't noticed that they were on the bicycle path, rather than the one for pedestrians. A cyclist rode up behind them, rang her little bike bell, and said, "Excuse me, but you're on the bicycle path."

Looking down at the markers, my friend saw that he was indeed trespassing. Muttering and grumbling, mostly out of embarrassment at his faux pas, he stepped off to let the cyclist pass. As she drew abreast, she turned and said, "You seem angry, would you like to talk about it?" "No." "Really, I'm sure you'd feel better if you talked about it." "No, I don't want to talk about it, go away." I guess she finally pedaled on her way, frustrated at being unable to "help" my friend have a nicer day. That's really being Too Psychological.

Conferences seem to encourage this behavior too. Professional types have all sorts of opportunities at such gatherings to stand around and play "My Psychology Vocabulary is Bigger than Yours." I'm sure I've never been guilty of this, but I've seen lots of other folks do it...

In fact, it might be a good idea for anyone fresh out of Therapy School to avoid conferences for a while, so she can have a chance to detox. It can take quite a while to get most of that stuff out of your system. All in all, I tend to lump being Too Psychological in with being Solemn and being Reverent - it's an OK place to visit, but I wouldn't want to live there.

I have enough trouble as it is. This year, through no fault of my own that I can determine, I was listed in my 30-year high school reunion roster as a "psycho therapist." I wasn't quite sure what to make of that, but it didn't sound very flattering. Maybe they know something I don't...

CHAPTER 10

Illustration

One of the best ways to keep the therapeutic journey from getting too solemn is to think of it as a dance we do together. Another good way is use fun illustrations instead of ponderous explanations to help clients Get what you're trying to communicate. Some illustrations I make up as I go along. Like this one that I thought of after working long and hard to help someone get over his pain from his mom's rejection of him. To little avail. He couldn't seem to stop Gathering Evidence of her coldness, even going so far as to bring a transcript of a conversation with her into group to prove his point. The other members agreed that she was pretty rejecting, all right.

So I made up this story. "Once upon a time there was a dairy farmer who had a herd of 100 cows. Ninety-nine of them gave rich, creamy, bounteous milk. But for some reason, he left them out in the pasture, mooing sadly because he was neglecting to milk them. And he kept the one cow who was dry in the barn and tried and tried to get a few drops out of her, and cursing and kicking and feeling bad all the while because he never got any. He would tell his family and his neighbors at length about this cow's stinginess, and about how unhappy he was with her. From time to time someone would ask him why he didn't use the other cows, but he maintained that this one cow had special milk, the only milk that would do the trick..."

By this time, my client was frowning, and the other group members were grinning broadly.   He Got It, however, and after a little grumpiness (I suppose you could call it resistance) he decided to try his hand at enjoying the milk from some of the many generous cows available in his present life.   When he left therapy, he presented me with a potholder in the shape of - guess what?   And every now and then I get a card from him with a cow on it, letting me know he's alive and well in happy-ever-after land.

This particular illustration has been enshrined in my practice as the "Cow Story," and I use it PRN, (as needed).   Most of the illustrations I employ, however, come from life experience, real encounters I've had with family, friends, clients, pets, books, etc.   Whatever the client is dealing with reminds me of a particular anecdote.   The association is effortless, and usually on target.

Suppose I'm working with a woman who's afraid of making a fuss, who wants to step out of a confining, people-pleasing role, but is scaring herself about doing that.   I want to illuminate for her the joys of being naughty or eccentric, so I'll likely tell her about the time I was riding the bus in downtown Seattle.   We were stopped in an area where a lot of street people lived.   As I looked out of the window at the folks waiting to board, I noticed one clean cut young man bent over at the waist tying his shoelace.   Behind him, an old bag lady was approaching, with her shopping bag in one hand and a closed umbrella in the other.

As soon as I saw the twinkle start to light up her eyes, I suspected what she was planning to do.   Sure enough, she came right up behind this fellow and goosed him with the end of her umbrella!   He shot up like a rocket and whirled around to confront his assailant, but she was waddling off down the sidewalk, cackling gleefully.   In fact there was quite a lot of glee going around the crowd there for a while, with one notable exception.

Illustration 89

Who could resist a story like that? You'd have to be pretty prim and proper not to want to turn out like that lady, I figure. That vignette gives all kinds of permission to have a grand old time raising heck whenever the chance comes along. Sure beats trying to be another Miss Manners.

Illustration works great to defuse sexual inhibitions too. As kids, we picked up, directly and indirectly, the views and attitudes of our parental units about sex. Not just our actual parents, but also grandparents, teachers, clergy, neighbors, even TV may have played parts in our gathering up a bundle of Rights and Wrongs about sex. So one of the targets to zero in on in order to enhance feeling happy with self and others in the sexual arena is the parental part of the client's personality makeup. See whether he will give himself some new permissions to enjoy his body and his sexuality.

Some time ago, I read a vignette about Dr. Mary Calderone, one of the founding mothers of sex education in our US of A. Evidently, she was bathing her young son and he was noticing his penis. Instead of being embarrassed and changing the subject, she apparently smiled and said to him "You're going to have a lot of fun with that some day." Fantastic! How many of us have been told with words or with behavior that our private parts were nasty, ugly, icky, etc?

A story like this can elicit any number of responses. That's part of why I tell it, to see how the client takes it in. Does she laugh? Does she cry? What does she say? Is she willing to treat the sexual parts of her body and personality in that accepting way? To deal with herself as Mary Calderone dealt with her son, and as she taught him to deal with herself?

Another of my favorite anecdotes came out of working with a delightful couple on their sexual differences. He felt more sexual inhibition than she did, and he wanted to become more relaxed and spontaneous. We did lots of archeology, exploring both of their backgrounds and early attitudes about their bodies and about sexuality.

We weren't quite getting to it, however.

Finally he said, "The thing about sex is, it's just not dignified!" DIGNIFIED? The three of us dissolved in laughter. When we could speak again, we had a hilarious time imagining what dignified sex would be like. Basic black with pearls? Tails? A butler announcing their arrivals after receiving their calling cards? How would they talk to each other? "How nice to see you again, madame, I trust you've been well"? "Very well, thank you, so good of you to inquire." What about the sounds and smells, would persons who were having Dignified Sex politely ignore them? Would formal invitations be required, with RSVP's?

Doesn't that present a marvelous image? I even have theoretical justification for having so much fun with clients. (I usually think of the theoretical justification after the fact, but that's OK.) I'll include it now, for those of you who care about such things. You see, the problem here was that he needed to change ego states, in Transactional Analysis lingo. Sex is a kid function.

What do I mean by that? Well, try to imagine Mr. Spock or Emily Post being spontaneous and playfully sexual. Tough, huh? The natural kid part of each of us is without inhibition until we start getting Trained. Training has its place, because we need to learn what behavior works in which settings - it's called having Social Skills. Trouble is, if we weren't raised by someone like Mary Calderone, and most of us weren't, we may get a bit over-trained as far as sex is concerned and become somewhat constricted in this area.

And then we're apt to have Great Big Feelings about that. "Ohmigosh, I've got Sexual Dysfunction!" You've probably already noticed that this is person-badness rearing its ugly head again, in yet another form. Insidious, isn't it? How can a guy relax and get spontaneous while being confronted with his badness? Forget it.

Illustration 91

I have to engage his kid part in order to correct over-training. In this case, we can laugh together and poke fun at the Sexual Dysfunction and Dignity monsters. And he can get a kick out of enjoying his plumbing and his playful intimacy with his partner. Monsters have no place in the bedroom.

Of course there's a considerable difference between a Dignity monster and an Early Sexual Abuse monster. Getting silly about sex will generally be way down the road for folks who were mistreated in this way as youngsters. First, they must lay a foundation of safety in the world and in therapy, which will be sturdy enough to support them in their battles with these Early Abuse monsters.

As a natural response to being misused, often by those they most loved and trusted, these folks have gotten some pretty dreadful ideas about themselves, others, and life. As you might imagine, these ideas are likely to be filled with badness and danger.

Here's a sampling. "Life is terrifying." "I can never know what to expect." "I'll have to learn to be very careful." "Men are dangerous." "Anyone I love will use me for their own ends." "I am damaged, not normal." "It's not safe to trust anyone." "Sex is scary." And the potent, underlying theme, "I am bad." Remember, feeling bad equates with being bad for a young child.

Helping someone with this early frame of reference to feel safer in the world and happier with self and others can be quite an under- taking. Part of the injury from being treated badly as a child by important adults is that the young person incorporates images of those attitudes toward her into her developing personality. These become important components of her attitudes toward herself as she grows older.

In other words, if she was treated with love and respect in childhood, she will mostly treat herself with love and respect as an adult. She will be apt to see that others continue to treat her lovingly and respectfully too. As a rule, if she was abused, she will abuse herself in some ways and allow others to do so too. If she was blamed, she will blame herself easily. If her parents gave her no slack, she will give herself none. And so it goes. But there's a catch here, and that is that most of the time these attitudes get even more punitive as they are taken in, so the grown person may be even harder on herself than others were on her as a child. No fair!

Thus, as I am telling her what a terrific partner she'd make, and gently inviting her out onto the dance floor, this punitive part of her may be telling her that someone like her doesn't deserve such a good time. That she's no good, could never learn the steps anyway, and would probably spoil my fun to boot.

Also, most adult survivors of sexual molestation learned to seal off their abuse experiences in some way, to protect themselves from trying to deal emotionally with something that, as children, they really couldn't. "I won't think about it," "I won't feel about it," and in some cases, "I won't remember about it." "I'll just put it all in this nice box and keep it in the back of my closet, where it won't bother me."

So she won't feel much like dancing. There's too much energy tied up in keeping that box where it belongs, out of sight and out of mind. She may be so depressed and hopeless that nothing, including dancing, sounds worth the effort.

Then it's a case of what do we do while we're sitting together on the sidelines, maybe getting ready to dance. We sort of hang out together while we Get to Know each other. She tells her stories, I tell mine. Only my illustrations now are gentle ones, stories of how loveable little children are, and how they should be cherished and protected. And how vulnerable they are. And how they are not bad, even if they think they are.

Illustration   93

We particularly get to know the child she was. Because even though my client may love other little ones, perhaps her own, she is probably estranged from the child she was. The child who experienced hurt, shame, confusion, fear, disappointment, and rage. She nearly always fears and avoids that child who exists in her memory. Where she would feel compassion and protectiveness for a daughter who'd been abused, she often wants nothing to do with her own child self.

She is estranged from an important part of herself, because she's scared to bring that box out of the closet. When she put it away, the monsters she stuffed into it were too big to deal with, and as far as she knows, they still are. So in order to work up the courage to bring it out and peek under the lid, she needs to call in reinforcements. She has to learn to be her own ally.

So we create images of this little kid. Was she blond or dark? What kind of clothes did she wear? How did she play? Are there any pictures of her around? What do they tell us? As we focus on getting to know this small human, the idea of pinning badness on her becomes more and more absurd. She's just a regular, lovable little kid who hurts and needs to be comforted, reassured, and protected, not avoided.

The healing that occurs as the adult client takes the risk of loving and welcoming this young part of herself is astonishing. She embraces herself as if she'd relinquished her little girl inside for adoption years ago and she and that lost child are now being reunited. She's giving up much of her self-badness.

In turn, the child part of her begins to feel more secure than she ever has before. Secure and safe enough to peek under the lid of the box. Because now she's teamed up with an adult (her present self) who loves her and can banish the monsters inside. This is the perfect adult for her, because no other adult in the whole wide world knows exactly how she feels, and can promise to be with her forever.

This relationship with herself is her primary relationship, much more crucial than hers with me, or with anyone else. Now that they are reconciled, the grown-up part of her can guide and support the child part of her in relearning about life and how to live it. Grown-ups can't eliminate pain from children's lives, but they can surround their children with love and hope while they journey through the ups and downs together. Isn't that all any of us can do for one another? It's a privilege, not a burden, and it's good enough.

With herself by her side, the client can now look the Early Abuse monsters straight in the eye and face them down, using anger, ridicule, humor - whatever works for her. She can turn them into harmless little Maurice Sendak monsters, like the ones in "Where the Wild Things Are." She can redecide all those harmful early script decisions about herself, others, and life. (11) Far out!

Of course, this reconciliation and building of a new relationship with self isn't accomplished overnight. It also isn't a logical, rational, process so much as it is an emotional one. The images of child and grown-up as parts of self just provide a cognitive framework to give structure and direction to the journey. And these images work, partly because they appeal to both the little person and the big person within us...

As we've been Getting to Know each other, and as I've been encouraging the client to nurture herself, I have at the same time been modeling how to do this by the ways in which I relate to her. Slick, huh? Naturally, the caring and support has to be genuine or her kid part will nix the whole deal. Remember, kids are smarter than shrinks.

Now we have a real therapeutic alliance going - Ginger Rogers and Fred Astaire, as it were. So we can start to really swing. Or maybe we'll put on our cowgirl boots and do some wild stomping around together. GET those monsters, ya!

CHAPTER 11

More Illustrations of Illustrations

I use illustrations a lot when I'm talking with clients about KIDS. I spend a lot of time normalizing the struggles between my clients and their younger generation. The parent-child dance is rife with possibilities for self-badness. Many parent-types are quite accepting of their children's negative feelings toward them, but not of their own toward their children, even though both are inevitable.

So I tell about my friend who had kids slightly older than my two. She endeared herself to me forever when she said, "Yeah, sometimes I think I'd adopt my kids out if I never got to see them when they're sleeping." What lovely permission to accept my own mixed feelings of frustration and joy in dealing with my sons.

Many parents carry Big Guilt about the ways in which they treated their offspring. (Not me, of course, but some parents...) When working with someone suffering from B.G. about parenting I want to teach them to give themselves some slack. A good way to do this is to tell about the time in my life when I was in my early twenties, had a toddler and an infant, and a husband who was quite ill. And how I would yell at my toddler and then feel terrible for having done so. One day I was saying to a neighbor, "I must sound horrible when I do that." "I don't hear a thing," she said. "No really, I'm sure I sound awful and mean." "I don't hear a thing," she repeated. I finally Got it. And so do clients, when I tell this story.

Another good way to undercut parental self-badness is to remind folks of the discrepancy between their human limitations and what they expect of themselves. It's impossible to conduct any relationship without conflict and error, especially one of a sort that you've never done before, like parenting. The alternative to imperfect relationships is to spend your life alone. Sit out all the dances.

Since the majority of us choose relating over isolation, then we have to decide whether to feel good about our relationships or to suffer about them. You've probably guessed which side I'm on. If feeling good about relationships requires some behavior changes, and you're having trouble effecting those changes, well, that's why nature made shrinks. To help ferret out the early script beliefs that are getting in the way.

Understand, I was all of 22 years old when I produced my first son. That's what you do, right, you get married and have kids? My assumption was that having reached that advanced age, I should be prepared for being a mom; after all, my mom had me at 20. And her mother had her at 18. Since I had expected extraordinary performances from myself up to that point, why should I be any different about judging my parenting?

Preposterous, isn't it? That's the sort of thinking many young folks do, though, and then they'll likely Gather more Evidence of their shortcomings. What a set-up. As an antidote, I strongly recommend bonding together with other new moms for preserving one's sense of perspective and one's sanity. And maybe one's sense of absurdity...

Of course, we sincerely want the best for our children. For their own sakes, and also because we can't help being somewhat identified with them. This identification blurs the ego boundaries between parent and child, and makes things get kind of gummy at times. Like when a parent is unknowingly achieving through the accomplishments of a child. I've suggested to quite a few moms that they take up soccer themselves if they seemed too caught up in their daughter's or son's performance.

But this individuation business is tricky sometimes. In fact, it may take 20 years or so to accomplish. Or may never quite get accomplished. With clients, I use the example of a person who was working on individuating from his own parents. One day he came in with a great story, which had turned on a Light Bulb for him. It seems that he had been on the phone with his mom, copying down a favorite recipe. As she was listing ingredients, my client heard his dad's voice in the background, "leave that one out, I don't like it..." I love this illustration of lack of personal boundaries between parent and grown-up child, and I use it frequently.

Usually, both parties are trying their best to get unstuck from each other. The process of getting this done, though, may not be a pretty sight. Thank heaven I went to that workshop years ago that was given by Natalie and Morris Haimowitz, two awesome therapists and trainers from Chicago. They lent us all an essential permission, which was this. "If something needs doing and you can't do it smoothly, then do it awkwardly, but do it!" And that's mostly how I've done it all right, awkwardly. Oh, well.

Another anecdote I use to help clients emancipate from their children is a story one of my shrink buddies told me. We were discussing what it was like around the family when the kids came home from college. "Rudolph seems to expect that it's going to be like Little House on the Prairie when the kids come home", she said. "But what really happens is that they fight with each other, and they hog the car and the phone all the time, and they want money, and they act like their family has leprosy and they feel deprived if they can't spend most of their time with their friends. I figure it's nature's way of letting us all know that it's time for them to move out."

One of the reasons I love this story is that it doesn't make anyone in the situation bad. It normalizes a regular human dilemma and really appeals to both the kid and the parent parts of most everyone. Makes it OK not to want to grow old together with your kids in the same household.

Another of my favorites, and I hope it will become one of yours, is an illustration derived from an old, old joke. I find this story very useful when a client is perched on the edge of leaving a difficult situation, such as an untrustworthy relationship, but is feeling stuck about getting on with it. At this point, the person will often minimize or temporarily forget about the destructive and hurtful aspects of the relationship. "It's not really so bad." Or, "It's probably the best I could do."

So I may say, "I want to tell you a story. One day the circus came to town and a guy went to see all the wonders it brought. Like lots of little boys, he had often dreamed of running away to join the circus. Wide-eyed, he asked one of the retinue, `What's it like to be in the circus?' `Well,' the fellow answered, `my job is a big one. I take care of the elephants. Want to see'?"

"`Oh boy, could I?' `Sure, come on with me.' So they strolled on over to where the elephants were standing around, being big. The keeper was showing them off to the townie when all of a sudden one of the pachyderms defecated all over him. He was covered with you-know-what. Aghast, the first man cried, `Are you OK?' `Oh yeah, this happens a lot,' responded the worker in a resigned tone, `it's part of the job.' `Good grief,' said the first man, `why don't you get another job?' The elephant keeper looked at him incredulously - `What, and leave show biz'?"

This story tends to disconcert, as you might imagine, and shake up even the most well defended frame of reference. The kid part of the client is at least strongly tempted to move out of a situation which they now may view as crappy. (I'm sorry, the devil made me say it...)

Not all illustrations are funny, however; some derive their power from human empathy. This is probably a good place to share one of my most poignant anecdotes. I use this one when clients are really struggling with self-badness and I want them to understand how vulnerable their self-esteem was when they were growing up.

One time I was washing my hands at a rest stop along the highway. In came a harried looking mom carrying an infant and followed by a little boy. Mom was obviously put out with the boy for some reason, and he was very distressed about it. As she went into a stall with the baby and closed the door, he stood outside crying and insisting frantically, "I a good boy, mommy, I a good boy!"

His anguish was wrenching. And my heart went out to both of them. I know what it's like to be trying to manage life and two little kids and be feeling overwhelmed and cross. I also know what it's like to be terrified, as that little guy was, that I've lost my place in the human race. Clients get it, too, and will generally use this story as permission to be more compassionate with themselves.

CHAPTER 12

Mental "Health"

Intriguing term...I confess that I tend to get up on my high horse about this one, because the way it's used insinuates people-badness. "That behavior is sick." "We don't have a healthy relationship." (What have you got, mumps?) "I'm here to get more healthy." You are not! You're fine as you are, you just are having glitches in your relationships.

We started using the sickness model in the first place because those famous early shrinks were docs. And it's right on for some things. In fact, some of the most exciting advances in the field are in the biological arena. Some stuff that we didn't dream was biochemical in origin responds to medication. Fantastic! More ways to enhance people's lives - better living through chemistry.

So some folks we see can accurately be called sick, or chemically out of whack. Talk therapy may or may not be helpful with them. Or may only be helpful in conjunction with medical therapy to put the person back in whack. Manic depressive illness is a good example of this.

The disease model, however, has gotten out of hand. It's been applied to all sorts of dif-fic-ulties people can have in their lives, as if unhappiness equated to illness. David Treadway, PhD, in his article "Codependency, disease, metaphor or fad," supports this view. He writes, "Most of us (therapersons) believe that the disease model can be a useful metaphor or reframe for many clients and yet we become uncomfortable when it is presented as scientific fact." (30, p.42)

Most clients, aren't sick. As in sicko. They're just regular folks and don't need to be cured of that. Mostly, they only need to change the way they're looking at things to get on with their lives. Granted, these changes may be profound, but they won't make them better people. Happier and more satisfied, but not Better.

So what's the deal? How come there's so much self-help literature out labeling darned near everything people are hurting about as a disease or an addiction? Codependency, for example, is a real phenomenon all right, but a disease, it ain't. It's another form of Big Person - Little Person relating. As Dr. Treadway states, "Currently, codependency is loosely used to describe the caretaking member of any complementary relationship." (p.41)

Folks who relate this way aren't different physiologically from those who don't. Codependency is a very normal outgrowth of the early decisions and early frame of reference of a kid who grew up with parents who didn't take care of business in some way. He becomes a caretaker. That's not a character flaw, it's what helped him cope. Now that he's an adult in the larger world, that way of coping is no longer suitable. He can turn it in on a new model, if he prefers. (If you're interested in a more thorough discussion of this topic, see my article "Loving Too Much - Disease or Decision?" in the October 1987 Transactional Analysis Journal.) (7)

I understand that giving up old attitudes and behaviors may seem really hard, and I also know that it usually takes a while. That's because the kid part of us that figured out that these were the ways to survive is a tough little bugger, and isn't about to give up crucial attitudes and behaviors until he's sure that's safe to do. Not just because some smarty-pants therapist says so. No way. (In Therapy

School, this is called Resistance, and is sometimes used as a disguised term for badness.)

This tough little kid part of the client is the reason you can't Make People Change. Anybody knows that kids are way smarter than shrinks. This is why therapists have to be tough. And real. Otherwise, they aren't trustworthy and that kid knows it. Does this sound like somebody sick? Or fragile? Have a clue.

And another thing. (This is a rather high horse, isn't it? Oh, well...) Addictions. What's the point in turning most everything anyone does rather excessively into an "addiction"? An addiction is a bio-chemical condition in which one's body has undergone changes that will cause a physiological crisis if a substance one has become addicted to is withdrawn. A physiological crisis is not the same thing as being stuck or as having feelings of loss. To quote Dr. Treadway again, "Skeptics have referred to this labeling of a wide variety of apparently dissimilar problems addictions as `the diseasing of America'." (p.40)

Merely being absorbed with or overdoing something is not the same as being addicted. Take soccer, for example. I adore soccer - have for 15 years or so. I'll do almost anything to get to participate as a player, fan, coach, or even referee. I'd rather be soccering than practically anything else at any given moment. I'd hate to have to give it up. I'm often preoccupied with thoughts of soccer. I have been known to bore others with soccer talk. I have asked therapy groups to switch meeting nights for soccer season. I even played soccer on my wedding day.

All of the above is old news to anyone who knows me. Some folks would call this an addiction, which would then turn soccer into something I ought to worry about, consider unhealthy, and possibly enter treatment for. Ragnar might even agree with these folks...(just kidding).

I prefer to regard soccer as one of the swellest aspects of my life, a fascinating eccentricity. And I have gone soccerless for extended periods, without having a physiological crisis. (I would probably be labeled catalog-addicted by these same folks. Even though I don't view catalog shopping in quite the positive light that I do soccer, I'm still not unhealthy for doing it. Somewhat poorer, perhaps, but not sick.)

Of course I know that the term addiction is not usually applied to soccer. Generally, it is now being used to refer to stuckness around unproductive relationships, eating habits, and ways of dealing with life. As in, "She's addicted to destructive relationships with men." Framing her dilemma in this fashion implies that there's Something Wrong With Her for getting into unsatisfying caretaking situations. "In some cases, labeling someone as a codependent may perpetuate the process of blaming in a new language," writes Dr. Treadway. (p.40) In the same issue, Carol Tavris, Phd, says, "...having a problem is not the same as being the problem." (The Politics of Codependency, p.43)

Seeing one's self as the problem sets up self-harassment. Now I don't know about you, but I have never found self-harassment to be an effective tool for facilitating change. Instead, it helps preserve the status quo. It also helps one stay in a Victim role, in this case the victim of addiction. Client as Little Person again.

Time for a re-frame. How about if the client is just seen as trying to get normal, OK, human wants and needs met? Is just regular, in other words. And is being hampered in this effort to be satisfied, and happy with self and others, by old business, by out of date script beliefs and options? Like "There's something wrong with me." Or "This is the best I can expect." Or "If I stand up for myself, I'll be left."

How about if each repeated stuck time is viewed as another effort by the client's kid part to resolve a familiar dilemma that didn't get resolved in childhood? Like how to have a successful and trusting relationship. Or how to feel good enough about himself that he knows he belongs in the human race. This way, there's no implication that the client somehow perversely wants to be unhappy, or can't get enough of being treated badly. "Recovery" is from early injury, not "illness."

I want to avoid the situation Dr. McDermott describes, "Psychology itself is getting brutally used by people in this culture. We pick a few words up from the lexicon and use them like weapons." (25, p.1) (against ourselves or others) So around my place we don't label stuff as healthy or unhealthy. I encourage folks to think, instead, about whether what they are doing is leading to satisfaction, and happiness with self and others. We do talk about addictions, but only when referring to substances that are addicting like tobacco, alcohol, cocaine, or valium. And we don't end up saying, as Dr Treadway finally does, "I'm not okay - You're not okay, but that's okay, because we're working on it together." (p.42) Aarrgh!

CHAPTER 13

Families of Shrinks, or, "Why Me?"

If we could choose our parents, how many of us would opt for shrinks? Oh well, we can't, so that's that. My kids were stuck with what they got and so was I. At this point, we all seem fairly pleased with the arrangement, but it hasn't always been a bed of roses. What relationship is?

So since I'm being rude enough to write a book and remind the members of my family again of their lot in life, I thought it might be nice to include a few words in acknowledgement of what they had to put up with. And maybe a few about what I had to put up with.

Some of my best friends are therapists, because helper-types are nice folks as a rule. From that standpoint, we're not bad to have as parental-units. Not all of our reasons for becoming helpers were unconscious, defensive responses to early dilemmas. Helping others solve life problems can be a legitimate way to live in this world, and be satisfied, and happy with self and others.

Being helpful feels good, whether I'm relating to a relative, a client, or a friend. Where most of us therapists get into heck with our families is when we forget to pay close enough attention to whether our current helpee, child, spouse, parent, or whomever, wants our help at that particular moment.

We may just be trying to be helpful, and they may be experiencing us as nosy and bossy. What a fix. Like when Ragnar's cooking, for instance. I tend to helpfully follow him around, cleaning up and putting stuff away slightly before he's done with it..."Out!", he exclaims, giving his best Scandinavian scowl and imperiously pointing his finger, "Or I quit!" Well gee, I was only trying to help...

Besides being too helpful, it's hard for us not to be Too Psychological after having been to Therapy School. So we tend to go in for Quality Relating, Talking It Out, and Family Meetings. Stuff like that. Kids have better things to do and respond by rolling their eyes and sticking their fingers down their throats. I tried to Promote Communication around our house for a while by holding Family Meetings. It was for their own good, of course.

Turned out that Wally and Beaver were much better at hating each others' guts during this era than I was at getting them to Relate. They turned the "Resentments and Appreciations" portion of our agenda into "Hatreds and Resentments," and there wasn't much we parental units could do about it.

Dr. Z has said that children of shrinks are quite well-defended. You'd better believe it! They know the score. One time I was hosting an informal meeting of shrink-types at my home. I invited the family to mingle at will. "No way," says Beav, who was about nine at the time, "someone will try to shrink me." "Don't be silly," I said, "Of course they won't, this is just a fun get-together."

Well, Beaver stayed holed up in his room until he thought everyone had left. One person was still saying his goodbyes, however, and so I introduced Beav to him. And you know what? I'll be darned if that guy didn't make an interpretive psychological remark to him about sibling rivalry! The look I got from Beaver was dripping with scorn and triumph. Gotcha!

I've had to put up with quite a lot from my family as well. Mostly bad puns, like, "This asparagus isn't even oedipal." And members of my extended family have been known to drop hints that I was way Too Psychological. I've always regarded such comments as uncalled for and rather rude.

Of course, when a family becomes as extended as mine, the whole spectrum of human behavior options is likely to show up. You see, through a series of divorces and remarriages, I ended up with nine grandparents. This can have its advantages, naturally, at Christmas and on birthdays, (mine), but can also prove confusing to a young child. It took me years just to sort out who belonged to who, and who used to belong to who, and so on.

My natural father, just to complicate things, evidently was married something like eight times, we're not exactly sure. My mother was number one, we do know that. They divorced when I was two, and I was adopted and raised by my mom's second husband, who's been a great dad. So I never really knew these potential step-moms, but I am certainly impressed by their numbers.

Even in my generation folks don't seem to stay put. Just when I think I've got the cast of characters down, someone changes the program. We've tried to deal with the confusion by differentiating between in-laws and out-laws, but it's still enough to make a person turn psychological in self-defense.

I also find it interesting that both of my sons have dropped the information that, they don't know why, but people seem to come to them with their problems, for some reason, and want to talk things over with them? Hmmm. All in all, I don't suppose having a shrink for a mom is any worse than having any other kind, as long as she has a sense of humor about it. And they've grown up with wonderful values - I'm quite proud of them. I suppose if Wally can stand having a shrink for a mom I can stand having a rock musician for a son.

CHAPTER 14

Techniques

Of course it isn't just families of shrinks who have to put up with us; our friends do too. As far as I know, I haven't lost any good buddies because of my occupational leanings, but some of them have let me know I'm pushing it. Like this one woman friend. She's a professional in another field, and quite a philosopher as well. It's been our custom to stay up into the wee hours arguing about the nature of mankind (more often womankind, actually), but anyhow, we have a great old time.

Early one morning when we were both struggling to stay awake and sound brilliant at the same time, I challenged the form, rather than the content, of her last point. She frowned, sat up straighter, and retorted loudly, "You're using Techniques on me!" Obviously, I had exceeded the bounds of good taste. My friend was making it clear that "techniques" belonged in the therapy room, period.

That's naive, of course. We all use Techniques on each other, Techniques are the stuff of human relating. Consider the Techniques of the infant - do you know any that are more powerful? The infant's problem-solving repertoire starts out with instinctual behavior. As she interacts with her parental units, however, she begins to notice what works with them and starts developing Techniques.

If we don't develop Techniques which work to get our human needs met, we fail to thrive, or may even die. From the moment of birth (and probably before) we are beginning to form our impressions and conclusions about life. The main impression for the infant is overall comfort or discomfort. Yum or ick. If she feels yummy, (dry, full, not too warm or cold, not over-stimulated or tired, etc) her body is relaxed. If she feels icky, (wet, hungry, in pain, too cold, etc) she becomes tense and begins to complain and protest.

These complaints are the beginnings of problem-solving behavior. When something is not right, she responds by doing something about that. Even though it's not deliberate, she is taking responsibility for getting what she needs. All sorts of things can happen next. Mom or dad may respond quickly, figure out what the problem is, and solve it with an attitude of patience and fondness. Great.

If she's lucky enough to be born into such an environment, which provides good enough problem-solving, then she will learn a very important sequence, one of the most basic human learnings. She will learn that when she has a discomfort, she needs to do something about it, and then most of the time she can get a satisfying response from others, and then she will feel good. Learning this sequence is crucial to living in this world and being satisfied, and happy with self and others.

Many factors influence this behavioral sequence, however. For cultural, climatic, physiological, emotional or other reasons, this sequence may fail to occur. For example, the child may have an illness or injury which prevents her from being made comfortable, even by the most capable and well-meaning caretakers. Or a parent may be trying to cope with several other problems, have too many balls to keep in the air. Or this child may be one of eight. Or mom, in trying to be a good parent, may be feeding her on a rigid schedule, so that whether baby is fed has little to do with whether she is hungry, or whether she has signaled discomfort.

So this infant may be forming some impressions about life that will not stand her in good stead later. Like, "I don't have take any responsibility for getting my needs met." Or, "People can't be trusted to help." Or, "Trying to get noticed doesn't do any good." Or, "Life is painful and lonely." Such conclusions would always fit the child's early situation, but probably would not prove very useful in the broader, grown-up world.

Those impressions created in infancy would not be verbal, of course, or clear, like the ones stated above, but would be more like bodily reactions - sort of like a somatic frame of reference. Does this child's physiology expect comfort and security most of the time, or not? The frame of reference about life becomes more verbal as the child herself does, and as she learns to tell the difference between herself and Mom, and between Mom and Dad, and so on.

OK, so here we have this kid who, from the start, has the job of figuring out how to live in this world (whatever the heck that is), and be satisfied, and happy with herself and others. These early script beliefs are crucial to the accomplishment of that task. And so is learning what Techniques work to gain that satisfaction and happiness.

If straightforward, direct Techniques work to please and influence her parents, she uses those. If the environment encourages or demands more round-about or complicated Techniques, well, then, she'll master those, if she can, and if they suit her. Outrage, flirtation, sadness, bribery, helplessness, guilt induction, reasonableness, sulking, teasing, are just a few of the Techniques that we inadvertently train our kids to use on us. Meanwhile, they, of course, are training us about which Techniques work with them.

A lot of folks get all worked up about the idea that someone tried to Manipulate them. Or put out at the suggestion that they might have stooped to trying to Manipulate someone else. Gee Willikers, what good are Techniques if you can't manipulate your environment with them? I figure we're all manipulating and techniquing around to beat the band, so why make a federal case out of it?

The deal in therapy, of course, is to trade in Techniques that don't work so hot at promoting satisfaction, and happiness with self and others, for ones that do; I'm OK - You're OK Techniques. So, again, the therapy relationship won't work as a tool for change if it's a Big-Person - Little-Person arrangement, because to the extent that it is, the Techniques modeled there will be one-up and one-down Techniques.

What are some examples of those? Well, helplessness, blaming, having to please others at all costs, guilt induction, intimidation, condescension, shaming, acting stupid, being unreasonably rea-sonable, ridiculing, being overly nurturing, and so on. These sorts of Techniques work at times in most families, so we're all familiar with them. Using any of the above perpetuates self- or other-badness or not-OK-ness in some form, however.

What to do? What Techniques can I draw on out of my Therapy School and personal life experiences to help the client exchange these badness-based Techniques for yummier ones, for ones that reflect and promote beliefs in OK-ness? Here's where the fun begins!

I guess that's the main thing they didn't tell me in Therapy School; how much fun the therapeutic dances could be! Lieberman, Yalom and Miles did clarify a lot about therapeutic dancing when they published their well-known study on encounter groups. I teach this material in my Group Treatment Training and would like to share it here.

In this study, the researchers demonstrated that what helped folks achieve positive outcomes had to do with certain qualities in the group leader's style, not with which branch of Therapy School she or he had graduated from. Positive outcome was defined as the amount of change participants achieved in variables like self-esteem, self-ideal discrepancy, interpersonal attitudes and behavior life values, defense mechanisms, emotional expressivity, values, friendship patterns, major life decisions, etc. [32, p.474]

A point here. This study was done with time-limited encounter groups. One could question whether those qualities that make an encounter group leader effective also make a psychotherapist effective. Dr. Yalom seems to think they do, [32, p.478] I do too. For support, I draw on my clinical experiences both as therapist and as client, and on the fact that I've done extensive Therapy School training with a marvelous psychotherapist, Bob Goulding, MD, who happened to be the leader of the encounter group in that study that had the highest positive outcome. So I think the study results fit therapists as well as encounter group leaders.

They showed that there were two qualities the leader couldn't have too much of: Caring (offering support, affection, praise, protection, warmth, acceptance, genuiness, concern), and Meaning Attribution (explaining, clarifying, interpreting, providing a cognitive framework for change; translating feelings and experiences into ideas). Caring - hmmm - the theraperson must show unconditional positive regard and respect for the client, I+ - Y+, not "caring" that features client as needy Little Person and therapist as all-giving Big Person.

Meaning attribution - the therapist must work from a cognitive framework that she can share with the client to help him understand himself and how he got to be the way he is. Theoretically, almost any framework will do the trick. I firmly believe, however, that this framework must rest in the I+ - Y+ concept, and that any of the subtle ways in which badness is held onto must be ferreted out and laughed out of existence. Otherwise, I don't see how one can achieve satisfaction, and happiness with self and others.

OK, so the therapist must come equipped with plenty of Caring and Meaning Attribution. She must also, according to the study, demonstrate just enough, but not too much, of two other qualities, Executive Function (setting limits, rules, norms, goals; managing time; pacing, stopping, interceding, suggesting procedures), and Emotional Stimulation (challenging, confronting, activity; intrusive modeling by personal risk-taking and high self-disclosure).[32, p.477] To me, executive function means the therapist must model assertiveness and protectiveness. This therapy setting is her territory, and she's in charge of maintaining it as a safe place in which to do therapeutic dancing.

If someone barges in selling flowers, she needs to barge him right out again. If one group client treats another with disrespect, she needs to model respect as she helps each look at what this interchange has to do with their therapeutic issues; with what they came in to change. At the same time, she needs to be in the background, to let the clients take charge of their own therapeutic progress - to follow their lead.

Emotional Stimulation - the therapist needs to remember which side of the couch she is on. This is not her personal therapy, she's the treasurer in this setting. So it won't work for her to try to push Big Feelings in the clients by being intrusive with her own. I think kid feelings are a different story, though, and that brings us back to where the fun begins.

So let's see here. We gotta provide a cognitive framework for the adult part of the client and caring, safety, and fun for the kid part. Using the therapeutic relationship as the tool. Okey dokey. Suppose one of the Techniques the clients learned to use to get along in her family was Helplessness. Without consciously intending to, or maybe even realizing it, she will bring Helplessness into our dance at some point.

Now, being a regular shrink-type, who got along in her early life by being Helpful, I could easily follow her lead by trying harder to be more Helpful. In fact, if I'm not on my therapeutic toes, I may still do that for awhile. Oh, well... Eventually, I come to, and change the music.

Here's where therapeutic nosiness pays off. If I've Gotten to Know her pretty well, I understand, cognitively or intuitively, which new record to put on. So I may respond to her Helplessness lead by totally forgetting how to be Helpful. "Boy, that's a tough problem you've got there, all right, beats me what to do". I call this Technique "Being Stupid." It doesn't come naturally to us helper-types who fear losing our place in heaven if we're not smart and useful, but it can be mastered, even if it wasn't taught in Therapy School.

And Being Stupid has many advantages. It's a way of letting the client know that (out of her awareness, of course) she sees herself as Littler and less capable than me. If I got too Helpful, I'd be agreeing with her and helping to undermine her self-coffidence. It's also easy and fun, once the therapist conquers her own terrible What If I'm Not Helpful Enough monster. It shifts the responsibility for problem-solving back to where it belongs, with the one who presented the problem. Finally, it's great modeling. Being Stupid can be varied as needed. Some other examples are Being Unreasonable, Not Being Pleasing, and Not Trying Very Hard. One counselor I knew in residential treatment was superb at Not Trying Very Hard. Understand that most of the clients in this setting were survivors of very tough early situations, and thus held on to their survival Techniques harder than most. So the shrink here has to be tougher than most.

Anyhow, this counselor's way of Not Trying Very Hard was to nod off if the client was too embedded in Helplessness as a Technique. He had it broken down into several steps. First, he would let his eyelids droop. If the client failed to notice and respond to that confrontation, he would let his eyes close and his head nod, jerking back up a few times, but finally letting his chin rest on his chest. If all else failed, he would snore.

It's important to understand that there is no ridicule of the client involved in something like this. If the client was sincerely struggling to change her frame of reference, the counselor would respond differently. In this case, that counselor was confronting the Learned Helplessness Technique monster.

You see, when a one-down Technique like Helplessness is adopted for survival, because it fits and works in the client's early life, the client experiences it as true about her, feels helpless a lot, and notes how others respond to her when she's this way. Since lots of folks will respond with Helpfulness, Helplessness can become a way to indirectly get stuff from others. A way with self-badness as its price. This by-product of Helpful responses from others is called Secondary Gain in Therapy School.

So she loses more and more coffidence in herself, and may see herself as impotent, rather than tough and smart. To be of any use to her in her journey to become more satisfied, and happy with self and others, the therapist must see her differently, and help her learn to laugh at and become bored with Techniques that undermine her sense of wonderfulness. This was one counselor's way of expressing his coffidence in her and was only one part of a relationship of mutual respect and caring.

Another therapist Technique for responding to client-presented Helplessness is more matter-of-fact. "Seems like you feel helpless about handling this yourself. Is that right? And I have the impression you'd like me to do something. What?" A straightforward confrontation like this will usually lead to a fruitful look at what's going on. And at what went on in the past to lead to this kind of dancing in the present. Insight.

The possibilities for changing the record are endless, and choosing among them is a matter of the therapist's knowing this particular client and knowing herself. And maybe of the phase of the moon, for all I know, I certainly don't always understand where these interventions come from. I could react to the Helplessness Technique by getting exaggeratedly Helpful till she made me stop. Or acting as if I never noticed the Helplessness at all. The crucial thing is that I stay out of a Big-Person role.

And what about some of the other relationship Techniques I mentioned? Like shaming, intimidation, ridicule, guilt induction, blaming, and so on. How do I change the music when these appear? Again, it depends on the situation. These Techniques only appear in a person's repertoire if someone else, perhaps a parental or grandparental unit, used them on him while he was growing up.

If they were used on him, he has learned to use them on himself. Or maybe he has learned to avoid using them on himself by using them on others. More often, both. So let's say the Blaming Technique monster rears its ugly head. Usually it's the Self-Blaming monster and it's threatening to gobble up what's left of the client's self-esteem today.

It may be hard to picture self-blame as a childhood survival technique, but it is. It's often scary and maybe dangerous for a kid to blame parents for his discomfort. So he'll blame himself. If important grown-ups are blaming him as well, or if he thinks they are, he'll incorporate their attitudes toward him into his developing personality, as part of his attitude toward himself. And if no one's around who thinks he's heaven's gift to their family, he may not incorporate much of a self-loving part. Ick.

As with any type of self-badness, the deal is to help the client get off his own case and on his own side. My main therapeutic Technique for accomplishing this is to start by getting on the side of the kid in the client myself. I just plain don't believe in kid-badness, and when it comes right down to it, most other folks don't either, except when they are dealing with the kid they were. That kid's another story.

It's pretty simple, the early injury was that the client failed to develop a part of himself that is self-supporting and self-nurturing. So he needs to do that now, and he can. In the process, the kid in him will shift out of the I- position, just like any little kid who's loved and nurtured will. It may take a while, exactly as it would if the client had recently adopted a child who came equipped with Self-Blaming monsters. That's all right, we have the time.

Clients will often say, "I don't know how to be accepting of myself." I may reply, "That's what you're paying your dough for. I know lots of ways. What you provide is the motivation and the guts." To start with, we get real familiar with who this kid really was. Same as in dealing with Early Abuse monsters, this child is often disowned and avoided.

So what did he look like? And just what were his supposed sins? And could all that nonsense really be true? And would the client say the rejecting and judgmental things to any other child that he says to himself? Of course not. So why pick on him? I may have the client put that imaginary kid on a chair in front of himself and say to that child what he's saying to himself inside his head. Bring it out in the open, where we can have a good look at it.

After the client and I have clearly pictured this little guy, who's maybe three or four years old with scuffed tenners and holes in the knees of his jeans, I will ask, "Are you willing to keep telling him he's awful and stupid? That he was so hard to live with that he drove his mother to drink?"

Even the most persistent Self-blame monsters cry "uncle" after a while when faced with having to be mean to a little kid like that. The client will eventually warm up to the remembered child and embrace him, so that his attitude toward himself becomes under-standing, loving, and protective. He will say things to the imaginary boy in the empty chair in front of him like, "You're a great kid. I love you and I'll never let anyone blame you again. I'll never leave you, either." He may even pick up this fantasy child and hold him and rock him, tears streaming down his face.

This kind of self-reclaiming experience is enormously healing, as you can imagine. Because the client is at once both the loving adult who is holding the child, and the hurting child who is being held. So he feels the wonder of loving and embracing himself at the same time that he feels the soothing of being protected and loved. Nifty, huh? So much for self-badness!

Of course a single experience like this doesn't banish all monsters forever and ever. It can, however, be an important turning point on the journey to satisfaction and happiness with self and others. After the client and I go through something as moving as this, each from our respective sides of the couch, our mutual dance becomes more joyous and free, like little kids skipping around the Maypole!

A final word about Techniques. One day while I was still in clinical training, I was bemoaning to Dr. Z. the fact that I didn't know enough Techniques yet. "You don't need to know more techniques," he said, "You just need to keep learning to listen." Boy, was he right! The better I get at listening (and other forms of paying attention) the easier my job becomes and the better I do it. If I'm paying good enough attention, the client will tell me exactly what she's about and what she needs from me.

CHAPTER 15

Homework

Some of the most fun I get to have as a shrink is when I assign homework. Not all of the therapy occurs in my office - things would go rather more slowly if it did. Clients often do a lot of smart thinking and making connections in between our sessions all on their own, of course. In fact, this is a good indication of their investment in the process. Some folks, though, don't think they are getting their money's worth unless they get to take home an assignment. And sometimes I can't resist.

Homeworks come in several varieties. There is the good old standby category, which most therapists develop to help folks deal with the sorts of problems many of us share. Like what we do about strokes. Stroke is the TA label for a unit of recognition, usually between humans, but not always. Stroking between human beings is a biological necessity, not a frivolous commodity. (24) We don't thrive without sufficient strokes, and can even do crazy stuff, like hallucinate, if we're totally deprived of human contact, as in solitary confinement. Yet our culture has evolved some pretty silly rules governing the giving and getting of strokes.

Some pretty stingy rules, if you ask me, like "Don't Ask for Strokes." Evidently wanting and seeking recognition from others is considered to be some sort of character flaw. We're also taught that if we have to ask, the recognition somehow doesn't count, so we shouldn't feel good about it.

Another common cultural rule is that "We Shouldn't Stroke Our-selves." Others won't like us if we feel too good about ourselves. Fooey! People won't like it much if we put them down in some way so that we can feel good about ourselves, all right, but that's different. Haven't you ever seen someone, big or little, full of themselves for some reason? You should have seen me when I scored my first soccer goal... Humans are downright adorable in that state, except to folks whose grapes may have gone sour.

And if, after all this, some recognition should happen to come our way, we're told that "We Shouldn't Accept Strokes." Instead we should pay for them by giving some back, "Thanks, yours is nice too," or we should point out to the giver why she's mistaken: "No really, it was nothing." In his book, "Scripts People Live," Claude Steiner gives a more complete description of this fix and how it came to be - look for the chapter on the Stroke Economy.(26)

So we gotta have 'em, but most of us are raised to avoid 'em. Where does this leave us? Hungry and cranky, that's where, just like any kid whose diet is severely restricted. And as Steiner points out, if our giving and getting of positive strokes (warm fuzzies) is curtailed, we'll go for the ones we are more sure of getting, the negative ones (cold pricklies). Cold pricklies nourish self-badness, warm fuzzies banish it.

So I end up doing a lot of stroking training in my work, since so many folks in our culture are somewhat Stroking-Disabled. Stroking disability interferes a bunch with satisfaction and happiness with self and others, as you might imagine, because exchanging recognition is one of the most important interactions humans can have with each other (and that includes us two humans on either side of the couch).

When I say something positive to a client about herself, I notice how she responds. Does her face light up? Does she keep right on talking as if I'd said nothing? Does she get tears in her eyes? Does she do a ritualized "thank you" or make some kind of disclaimer like, "It was really easy," to let me know that whatever I'm recognizing her about is unimportant? Sound familiar?

If the recognition didn't seem to soak in, I'll interrupt and ask her about it. "What did you say in your head just now when I commented that you were a good parent?" Her internal critic has usually deftly intercepted the stroke with some thought like, "If she really knew all the parenting mistakes I'd made, she'd never say that," or "She has to say stuff like that, it's part of her shrink role." Presto, no feel-goods from that stroke, more going hungry and more self-badness.

The content of her inner dialogue provides useful clues to early scenes with parental units, and to family norms about self-esteem and closeness. Controlling strokes is one of the unconscious ways people control the level of intimacy in their lives. Suppose the aforementioned client let herself really take in my appreciation of her parenting? Ohmigosh, she would be letting me really count, really affect how she felt about herself. In doing so, she would be making me into a more important person in her life, a person who could have an impact, whose opinion mattered to her. Maybe she's not feeling ready to do that.

Whatever she's doing with me about strokes, she's also doing out there in the big world, and that behavior is making a difference in her level of self- and other-yumminess. So she may well decide she'd like to learn some more useful stroking behaviors, some which promote happiness with self and others. Here's where the homework comes in (you thought I'd forgotten, I'll bet).

One of my most favorite homeworks is an old TA standby, the Count to Ten homework. It goes like this, whenever you notice that someone has given you a positive stroke, you maintain eye contact with the person and internally count to ten before responding. Sound easy? It ain't! Because what you are doing is giving up your usual ways of controlling the impact you let someone have on you, and that turns out to be darned uncomfortable.

Like, you might blush, or even get tears in your eyes. Try it, if you don't believe me. In fact, one client did this homework for a week and found it so disturbing he came back the next week and negotiated with me to only have to count to seven. (He wanted five, I went for eight, and we compromised.) Now this was a very together guy who had great social skills, so that gives you some idea of the impact human recognition can have if we let it.

Because of the popularization of the term strokes, some folks tend to dismiss the concept as over-simplified. That's a shame. The client's behavior around human recognition provides rich information to the clinician about his family of origin, his existential position in life, his frame of reference, and how he stays stuck in self-badness. And stroking behavior is a swell place to intervene, because it's easy to spot, fun to play with, and makes an immediate difference in how much the client enjoys his day.

Probably the most frequent homework assigned around my place is Talking it Over. You see, a client will tell me at great length how she feels about, what she fears from, what she wants from, someone important in her life. "Have you told her this?" I ask. Blank look. Then she may light up and exclaim, "What a novel idea!"

Or she may tell me all the reasons why she couldn't possibly do that, most of which fall under the heading of "I'd be scared of what she'd do." A lot of them sound kind of nuclear too, like "she'd explode," "she'd melt," or "she'd fall apart." At this point I assure her that I have yet to see anyone do any of these things, in my office or elsewhere, even though I've known many who feared that they might. In Therapy School, such fears would be called Grandiose. (Exaggerated.)

Many of the reasons given for not Talking it Over are antiques. Like "she wouldn't listen," "she'd ridicule me," or "she'd leave." These are probably reactions the client encountered as a kid, and has grown to expect from folks whose responses matter most to her. So she has the conversation in her head, decides how it would turn out, and then has feelings that go with those fantasies.

But this is now, not then. Remember "To live in this world...?" There's a whole lot of difference between the past and the present. For one thing, the current friend probably bears very little resemblance to the parental unit in question. For another, the client isn't a kid any more, and has way more power and options, now that she's a grown-up. If the friend does respond in some tacky way, the client can train her or trade her or do whatever else she needs to do to continue being satisfied and happy with self and others.

Another common excuse for not Talking it Over stems from a boundary confusion - "I don't want to make her feel bad." Or "I don't want to hurt her feelings." The great "make-feel" controversy! Technically speaking, my client can't make her friend feel bad, because her friend's emotions depend much more on what my client's behavior means to her than on what the client actually did.

Here's an illustration. Once a woman related to me how her father had flown in from another state to personally reprimand someone who had offended her. "How did you feel about his doing that," I asked? "Wonderful, of course, it meant that he loved me," she replied, amazed that I would even ask. How could I imagine her feeling otherwise?

"Well," I said, "if his coming to your rescue like that had meant to you that he was an interfering busy-body who didn't think you had the brains to manage your own affairs, it's possible you'd have felt differently about the interaction." So it isn't strictly the other's action that makes one feel something; it depends more on what the behavior means to the person and on what she wants at the time. In other words, the above client "made herself" feel good about what Dad did, and she could just as well have "made herself" resent his part in the dance.

Unfortunately, we are usually raised to believe that we make others feel good or bad. "You make me so mad when you do that!" Hmmm. Actually, it's probably Mom's belief that the kid is being disobedient in some way that makes her mad. Or maybe it's a last straw. Or whatever. In any case, "I get so mad when you do that," is more accurate and takes responsibility for the emotion, rather than giving it to the kid.

Finding out that people (like moms, for instance) usually get mad when you act a certain way is important learning for a kid. He needs to learn to take others into account. It's another story entirely for a kid to get the grandiose idea that he has just ruined Mom's day. He's not in charge of her deriving happiness and satisfaction out of life; she is. But he may grow up thinking her emotional welfare depends on him. No fair.

Another statement that many of us cut our teeth on (and probably passed on to our kids) is, "You really hurt me when you do that." Most of the time, that translates to, "I get mad as heck when you do that, Buster!" But the person doesn't acknowledge his anger, maybe even to himself; "hurt" seems more acceptable. Trouble is, "hurt" in this usage is guilt-inducing. The kid is likely to believe he's done Mom or Dad injury, and is therefore bad, rather than that he can expect some people to get ticked when he does that particular thing.

In case you're preparing for self-flagellation, because of having taught your own kid in this way, I suggest you put your whip back in the closet. This kind of parenting has been culturally taught for a long time. Better boundaries are easy to learn. I teach folks about them all the time, because most everyone who walks through my door is taking too much responsibility for some stuff and not enough for other stuff. Such fuzziness preserves script beliefs and people-badness.

So I offer people the chance to trade taking responsibility for someone else's feelings in for having respect and regard for others' feelings. Just because I don't make you feel a certain way, doesn't mean I have no influence or impact on you, and I do need to acknowledge that. I+ - Y+.

Another of my favorite homeworks is Noticing. Noticing is designed to bring new information into the client's frame of reference. See, all those beliefs about self, others, and life make a neat little package, and a good deal of what she pays attention to will have been unconsciously pre-screened to reinforce those views. So she may notice, for example, whatever data in her day to day life that supports her belief that people are unfriendly, and not notice any that would challenge that conviction. I call this unaware filtering Gathering Evidence.

Her homework, then, might be to Notice the whole picture. Notice people noticing her. Notice what she says to herself when they do, and how she feels after saying that. Notice what she does, and what responses she thereby invites back from others. Even though she hasn't yet changed any outward behavior, she has interfered with her usual Gathering of Evidence.

If she's skilled enough at Gathering of Evidence, she can support virtually any conclusion about life and people. We all can. Creative Noticing, however, brings in new information and invites the person to notice what the real, present world she lives in is like. Often, it looks pretty different from the one she grew up in and thought she was still living in.

Following a certain amount of Noticing about self and others, the client likely will want to change something he's doing out there in the world - something that's interfering with his getting what he came into my office for. Like the fellow who Noticed that he kept picking on his partner for her various character flaws and generally making himself unpleasant to be around. Natter, natter, natter. He could see that this nagging might easily lead to his losing her, which he certainly didn't want, but which would really reinforce his script expectations about what he deserved.

So he asked for some powerful homework he could do to cure himself of this obnoxious behavior. This guy was an ex-marine. I knew him well enough to be pretty sure he wouldn't be satisfied with any namby-pamby homework like "oops" - it would have to be an assignment for a Real Man. "OK," I said, "whenever you find yourself doing it again, drop for ten. It doesn't matter where you are or who's around, make sure you do it immediately."

He loved the idea, and bragged in his next session about how he had done ten pushups in his best suit downtown in front of I. Magnin. I guess if you're going to be doing pushups in front of I. Magnin, it's best to be properly attired...

This fellow traded in self-harassment for silliness. And built up his triceps, to boot. He couldn't fail, because if he hadn't done it, or even if he'd forgotten about it entirely, that would just have been more grist. Outrageousness is important here. The more outrageous the homework, the more that client's kid likes it, and the more apt he will be to give it a try.

Like one couple I was seeing, who wanted to stop their unproductive fighting and do stuff together that was more fun. They had already progressed from hindsight to middlesight. That is, one or both of them could now realize that they were Doing It Again right in the middle of the fray, instead of afterwards. They wanted something to do right then, as soon as one of them Noticed their familiar behavior.

Right. Well, let's see, these folks were much too serious and reasonable, and they were also geriatric athletes, like me. What would be a sufficiently unreasonable intervention to break up the fight? "How about this," I suggested, "as soon as either of you realizes you're at it again, you begin shouting `Oh no, we're doing it again!' and run out the door and clear around the house, shouting the while. The other one must do the same, only he or she has to circle the house in the opposite direction."

Since their house was large, I imagine they got quite a few aerobic points for that homework, along with some new topics to discuss with the neighbors. "What the heck were you guys doing, anyway?" "It's OK, we're in therapy..."

I assign a great deal of homework that's designed to improve my client's relationship with his kid part. So his kid learns that this world and the people in it are pretty swell after all, and that he can probably relax and have a good time. Like with the couple I was seeing who were buying their first house together. Their plans did not include future offspring, so the new house was relatively small and just completed. A clean slate. Too clean - they didn't know where to start in the process of making it into a home.

It turns out neither of them had gotten to have their own room as children. In different ways, each had grown up in rather bleak and stark circumstances, so the kid part of each of them expected to live bleakly and starkly ever after. Together, we devised a fantastic plan. This couple would pretend they were adopting two orphans, kids who had lived through some tough times, and who were adept at Making Do and Going Without. And who were pretty skeptical of nurturing treatment from grown-ups.

Adoption, you understand, is quite an undertaking. These two folks had a fine time figuring out what would be welcoming and reassuring to these imaginary kids (who were really parts of themselves, of course). They knew that they had to go slowly, because the kids needed time to accept and believe in the reality of this new family. Believe that someone was actually going to create an environment that would be especially for them. They could know what they wanted and ask for it - no strings.

Kids who survive awful childhoods are Wanting Impaired. Such children were so busy developing Techniques and dances to survive that their Wanting organs got squished. So you can't just say to kids like that, "You can have whatever you want, tell me what that is." They may not have a clue. They may only know what they don't want - getting hit, for example. It's a matter of priorities.

So I worked with this couple first of all on creating a generic Kid house, comfortable, not too orderly or fragile, and above all, with pets. Then they had to spend lots of time Getting to Know these two "orphans" and building trusting relationships with them. As the "kids" relaxed, their Wanting organs gradually puffed back up to normal size, and they could tell the "adults" what sorts of stuff made a home comfy for them. Not that they always got that particular item right away, adults being the practical sorts that they are, (and being in charge of the dough) but at least they all had guidelines to work with - ways to please each other and themselves.

Feel free to borrow any of this homework that appeals to you. I realized after working with this couple that my kid part has always had a hankering after built-in bunk beds, so I've put them on the remodel list. We all have our own kid ideas about what makes a real swell bedroom; maybe for you it's an attic with slanty walls and tiny print wallpaper. You choose.

CHAPTER 16

*Redecision**

---

*This creative and effective therapeutic process, a combination of TA theory and Gestalt techniques, was developed by Bob and Mary Goulding. For a more complete understanding, read some of their books listed in the bibliography. They're great! (11,12,13)

Here's how I use Redecision Therapy in my practice. As already mentioned, kid script decisions in response to early trauma can determine the fabric and quality of the person's life from childhood on. Here's an example. One client came to me because she felt half alive. She was alcoholic, but had stopped drinking many years ago. Even after taking charge of her drinking, she continued to live her life numbly; everything was a huge effort, and what she accomplished brought little satisfaction.

She had few friends, partly because finding them seemed like so much trouble, and partly because she would write them off as soon as they disappointed her in some way (which all friends do, of course, at some time or other). You can go through a lot of friends that way. She had never had a successful intimate relationship, she didn't see the point.

She was somewhat depressed, but mostly just shut down. Existing, rather than living. She had an suspicion, though, that there might be more to life than all this, and so she came into therapy, a bit cynically, to see. We met weekly for some months, Getting to Know each other. Our relationship, naturally, was hard work for her and not too satisfying, just like the others in her life. We discussed this and she made some changes, but didn't really move from her "numb" position.

She left therapy for a while, and then came back after a year or so, ready to give it another try, difficult as it might be. Well, eventually she told me about an event when she was about five. She had accidentally been severely burned, and had been hospitalized for quite a while afterward.

Alone. In those days, parents weren't usually allowed to stay with their kids in the hospital. Also, she had a brand new sibling at home, as well as a couple of older ones - Mom had her hands full. And Dad traveled a lot.

Do you know how they treat severe burns? In order to prevent debilitating scarring, the scabs that form on the burn have to be periodically scraped and peeled off. It's excruciating. It's not only excruciating for the patient, but also for the folks who have to inflict the treatment, naturally, especially if the patient happens to be five years old. Her memory is that she was told not to cry.

So here she was at five, busily doing her regular kid stuff and having a pretty good time, by and large. Then, through no one's fault, the rug was pulled out from under her and her world turned upside down. All of a sudden she was alone in a strange place, terrified and in extreme pain, without even the capacity to understand that it would be over eventually. And she was afraid to protest.

Possibly she told herself not to cry, or possibly her caregivers told her, but in any case, she tried her best not to - tried to marshall her five-year-old tools for dealing with the situation. As best she could, she numbed out. Her Rage and Terror and Pain monsters were too big to face. They were even too big for the grown-ups in the situation to face.

And she stayed numbed out. She drew some understandable but fearsome conclusions about life at this time, and made some important decisions. "Life is very hard and unsafe." "I'll never let myself get excited again, because I could get a terrible surprise." "I'll never depend on anyone again, because they can desert me when I need them the most." "The only tolerable way to deal with life is to be numb."

These early conclusions and decisions were still determining her life experience. They were interfering with her options for satisfaction and happiness with self, others and life. An absolutely crucial point here: It was not the fact of having been burned per se that was causing her problems in her adult life. These script decisions and conclusions were the culprits.

A good thing, too, because anything that one has decided as a kid, even out of awareness, one can re-decide later if that seems like a good idea. Mostly, that boils down to whether it seems safe (or sometimes, whether the old belief now seems ridiculous). So that's why psychotherapy works. We don't have to go back and change the past, fortunately. We therapersons, using the therapeutic relationship as a tool, can help clients redecide about self, others, and life. (11) They can then get on with Living in this World, Being Satisfied, and Happy with Self and Others.

These new decisions will be more useful and appropriate in the light of current events. They will also offer a wider range of options for problem-solving than a kid can draw on. Numbing probably has its uses for an adult, but they are limited. In fact, numbing out can positively get in the way of feeling joyful, I've noticed. Besides, we need our feelings, even when they aren't pleasant, to tell us what's going on with us.

So you can see that folks aren't doomed to live awfully ever after, just because they may have been the childhood victims of intentional or unintentional trauma. We all have the power to change our lives.

Obviously, there was never anything wrong with or bad about this child, or about the adult she grew up to become. Nor were the other actors in her drama bad. My hat goes off, in fact, to anyone who can work with burn patients; it must take a special kind of guts. I have enough trouble dealing with emotional scabs and scar tissue.

Like most people, all these folks were just doing the best they knew how, and coping by using the tools they had available then. When this woman entered therapy, she definitely believed in her own self-badness, and she wasn't too keen on others, either. She was sure that her lack of enjoyment of life was just somehow perverse, and she hoped that maybe I would help her shape up - help her become a better person.

Pretty silly, isn't it? She certainly was never bad, she was just holding on for dear life to some understandable but not very useful beliefs. Changing such beliefs may take quite a while, since the kid part of the client has to really be convinced that letting go of them is safe now. It may even be expensive and seem scary. But not changing them is even more costly.

And I can't just say to a client, "Well it's no longer appropriate to see things that old way, so you can stop now and believe only positive and beautiful things from here on out." The process doesn't work that way. If it did, nature wouldn't have needed to make therapists, because regular folks would figure this all out on their own and change it. Trading in out-moded decisions and Techniques is an emotional and irrational deal." They may not be the greatest, but they've gotten me along so far, and I'm not at all confident that the new models will."
Sort of like how I've approached this computer I'm presently attached to by my fingers. Skeptically, warily, cautiously, and definitely irrationally. "Oh yeah? Prove it to me! Go ahead, convince me that this new-fangled way of doing things will work better." I found I was secretly delighted when a power surge put this baby out of commission for a while. The frustration of having to

delay my writing schedule was more than offset by getting to say, "I told you so, I knew they couldn't be trusted..."

The client is taking her own time to shift; to redecide. Her pace-setting needs to be accepted by herself and by her therapist, not labeled as Bad Resistance, even though it's easy to see it in that way. I still slip into that mode occasionally myself: "That stubborn client! Why won't she change? Can't she see I'm only trying to help? It's for her own good, after all..." Embarrassing, but true. In my own wish to be Helpful, I lose sight of the fact that her kid part is wise, and is in charge here.

Once this woman started to dance, she really went for it. She also started singing, got a new job, and began to make lots of new friends. She didn't kick them out of her life, either, when they let her down; she learned to patch things up and go on. She even learned to be excited about stuff like Christmas. I'd say she's now living about as happily ever after as most anyone. Fragile? Her? No way!

CHAPTER 17

Talking to Chairs
(and other weird stuff we have clients do)

I allowed at the beginning that psychotherapy is a peculiar way to spend your time. Since you're still with me, I guess it's probably OK to let on just how peculiar it can get. The strange rumors you've heard are true - we do get people to talk to chairs.

Hardly anyone in my practice squeaks through their therapy without having to go through this ordeal. Early Life monsters can be vanquished without talking to chairs, but such conversations usually speed up the process a bunch. Besides, I've done more than my share of talking to chairs as a client, and if I had to, I don't see why anyone else should get out of it...

It's not my fault; Fritz Perls started it. Blame him. Actually, he had a really good idea. Why not bring the internal conversations we all have in our heads out in the open, where they can be worked with? There's important therapeutic info inside that skull, but it's all a secret as long as it stays in there.

Now, the client can report on these internal dialogues to the therapist, but that's a whole different experience than if he acts out the dialogue. Acting it out makes it much more immediate and real. How does the client act it out? By talking to chairs, of course.

Here's how it works. First, you gotta have a chair. You probably have

139

one or two sitting around your place. Then you gotta have a dilemma. That's easy; the clients are happy to provide those - a conflict with a supervisor, for example. Client starts describing it in session. Therapist says something like, "Imagine your supervisor is sitting here in the room right now in that empty chair. Tell her what you really wanted to say but didn't. As if she's actually sitting there."

Now that's kind of weird, right? Talking to an empty chair? It works, though, because pretty soon the client becomes absorbed in the dialogue just as if the supervisor were there interacting with him. And then the client feels the emotions he would feel in the actual situation, and acts like he would if he were really at his office, and so on. In other words, the role-play has a lot of reality to it.

This element of reality is important, because with it there's whole bunches more information available in the room than if the client were simply describing the situation. Instead of talking about something that occurred out there in the real world in the past, he's experiencing the conflict in the present in the therapy setting. The feelings he's having and what he's doing inside his head can all be explored and used.

Talking to chairs provides a great avenue into redecision. (11) If the client is struggling with his boss, and feeling stuck, chances are that this drama echoes an earlier conflict in the client's life which was never resolved. (It probably echoes one in the boss's life too, but she's not the client here, so we don't concern ourselves with that.) And because the client's embroiled in it right in the therapy room, the therapist can get at the early dilemma.

Like this. "What are you feeling toward your supervisor right now?" "Anger." "And what are you saying in your head about her, and about you?" "She's not being fair, and there's nothing I can do to please her." OK. "When you're a kid, feeling angry like you are now, and saying in your head, `She's not being fair; there's nothing I can do to please her,' what's the scene?"

Usually, the client will associate to a scene when he was a child dealing with an important adult in his life, maybe Mom, in this case, or Grandma, or a teacher. Aha! Now the therapist has the real stuff to work with. The supervisor is removed from the empty chair and Mom is put there. "Be the age you were in the scene and talk to Mom about how you can't please her."

With the therapist as director, the client re-enters the early drama, generally moving back and forth between his seat and the empty chair as he acts out both roles. He's showing the therapist and himself one of the conflicts he carries around in his head - how he talks to himself. He's also illustrating whatever he decided about self, others, and life at the time, such as, "Since I could never please her, there must have been something wrong with me. Maybe if I try harder and harder, I'll finally get her approval and then I'll be OK."

So that's probably how he's spent much of his life, trying and failing to please important women in his life, confirming his badness and aloneness in the world. Even though he's done this over and over, it's not sick or an addiction. He's still trying to please Mom and be OK in the world - nothing wrong with that; it's pretty regular. It's normal to want those things (diagnosis, human being).

But the deal is, unless he gives up symbolically trying to change Mom in the past by trying to please unpleasable women in the present, the dance will keep turning out about the same, preserving his script beliefs intact. That's one thing talking to chairs is good for. While the client is back in the early scene, feeling and viewing things as he did then, I'll see whether I can help him shift positions in some way. Whether he'll draw on his spunky kid energy to stand up for himself with Mom and get himself out of the fix he's in.

Will he take back from her the power to rule on his worth? Will he say something to her like, "Just because you're so fussy doesn't mean there's anything wrong with me. Lots of other people love me and

I'm paying attention them, not to you." Note that he's not trying to make her into a more giving mom. He's changing what he can change: his responses; his script decisions.

Or if he won't budge from his original position, I may just ask him to acknowledge his stuckness by saying to Mom in the chair, "I'm going to keep feeling bad until you tell me you are pleased with me." Of course, he may not quite be able to force these words out. That's fine, too, because then he'll have to chose whether to continue to feel powerless and admit that it's a choice, or stand up for himself and feel good.

These role-plays may be nearly as real to the client as the original experience was, even though the chair is empty. The client feels the emotional power of that early encounter, (is really in his kid part) and uses that energy to change his out-moded beliefs about his own badness and about how to interact in life.

It's a little tricky. See, what's in the chair is really a self-harassing part of the client, not Mom or supervisor. That self-critical part may have been modeled originally after Mom, but it's now a part of the client and thus is within his power to change. What a deal - it works great!

You can put just about anything on the chair. In my forays on both sides of the couch, I've seen houses, penises, dogs, wicked step-parents, cars, Uncle Sam, black slimy parts of self, and many other items, too numerous to mention, put on empty chairs. More grist.

And we do other weird stuff besides talking to chairs - taking fantasy trips, for example. Fantasy in any form is a most effective therapeutic tool. The fantasy might be of an early scene, or it might be made up to suit the occasion. Like the group member who decided as a kid when his dad died that his life would be lonely and bleak ever after. One day he was describing his feelings about an impending break-up with his partner. He was really down.

One of the other groupees said, "Mortimer, it sounds like you expect to end up in a cold hotel room with a cot and a bare light bulb dangling from the ceiling." This possibility seemed pretty remote, considering Mortimer's circumstances, so we had a fine time fleshing out this stark fantasy. All of us joined in, even Mort, and added a faded, scratchy army blanket, cockroaches, a dripping sink in the corner (cold water only, of course), a blinking neon sign reflecting in the filthy window, scritchy linoleum, peeling wallpaper... And it was raining outside, of course.

After a while this got too absurd for Mortimer, and he burst out laughing at the Ending up Alone in Bleak Circumstances monster. It shriveled right up and crawled pitifully across the floor and through the crack under the door, never to be heard from again.

Or how about the rickety glider fantasy? Once I had a client who had built her own hang glider a few years before coming in to see me. Evidently, it had an annoying habit of shedding parts while aloft. So far, none of the essential parts had fallen off while she was in the air, and she seemed to think the whole situation was pretty funny.

She pooh-pooed my response that this was self-destructive behavior that could get her hurt or dead. So I asked her to do a fantasy. She had a little three-year-old niece she adored. I told her to imagine that it was a nice summer day, and she was going to take this child for a ride with her in the glider. She frowned. Ignoring the frown, I said, "And say to her the things you've been saying to yourself about how it's a little rickety but that's part of the fun, ha, ha." "No", she protested, "I couldn't do that!" "Why not?" "Because I love her and I wouldn't want to take the chance that she might get hurt." "Oh," I said with a smile. She Got it.

As long as we're already aloft, I'll tell about another fun fantasy. One client scared himself a lot about flying. This became an acute dif-ficulty when he wanted to take a vacation that featured two trans-

Atlantic flights. I asked him to imagine that he was boarding the airplane.

What was he feeling? Anxious. Heart pounding, short of breath. What was he saying inside his head? "I'm scared because I'm not in charge of this plane." Huh? "Are you a pilot," I asked? "No." "Well, thank heaven you're not in charge of the plane! Let's hope whoever's in charge of the plane is a licensed pilot with lots of experience!" After we stopped guffawing, we figured out some homework for him to do whenever he boarded an airplane.

He was to take the time to look over the cockpit carefully, noting who was in there and what their job was. Should the cockpit be empty when he got on the plane, he was to ask the flight attendant for the pilot's name and experience. If possible, he was to arrange an opportunity to go forward and see for himself. This worked swell, because every time he did it, or even thought of doing it, he started laughing and stopped scaring himself. Ta da!

Like illustrations, fantasies aren't always funny. I'll always remember one especially moving fantasy I structured for a client whose grandfather had been very sexually inappropriate with her. Sometimes an adult who had a relative take advantage of his or her caring and trust as a child to "merely" sexualize their relationship has a harder time dealing with it than does someone who was raped or otherwise badly hurt physically.

When I use the phrase "sexualizing the relationship," I'm referring to situations in which sexual boundaries are being violated in somewhat subtle ways, ways that may be harder for the child to protest, because the abusiveness is less clear. Things like fondling of breasts or genitals in the context of bathing or putting the child to bed.

In such a case, even though it's still abusive, there's no brutal event to recall that would explain to the client her confused emotions.

Since she probably wants to pretend the whole thing never happened anyway, this provides an excuse to stay out of touch with her feelings about having been used in this way. This particular client knew she ought to be outraged at her grandfather, but cared about him a lot, and found it easier to be mad at herself.

I asked her to fantasize being her grandfather, walking into her bedroom as he usually did "to say good night." I asked her to look through his eyes and see herself at thirteen, just starting to mature. What must she have looked like to him? How must he have regarded her? What would he have been thinking and feeling?

As soon as she did that, she became enraged on her own behalf. For the first time, she was absolutely clear that what he did was selfish and totally inappropriate. And that she was not bad. As she felt protective toward her thirteen-year-old self, she stopped confusing herself about that relationship and changed the hurtful conclusions she had originally drawn from it about herself and about trusting. And is now living quite happily ever after. Powerful, huh!

Mary Goulding, MSW, does marvelously creative work curing phobias through the use of fantasy and imagery. It was after watching her work with small animal phobias at Western Institute for Group and Family Therapy that I devised this fantasy to use with a client. This fellow had survived an extremely violent and frightening childhood. He had lots of friends and functioned well in the world, except that he was at times quite anxious.

One day he told me of a recurrent dream. He was a little guy in his bedroom at home. He could see through the doorway and into the living room, where a large rat with scary teeth was crouching. It would see him and start to come after him, at which point he would wake up, terrified and sometimes screaming. Now, there were a lot of ways I could have gone with this dream, especially since I knew so much about his history.

He'd done a lot of early scene work already, though, so I decided to play with the dream, in the hopes that he would gain some control over it. So I asked him to close his eyes and put himself back in the dream setting. I pointed out that since this was a fantasy, not a real dream, he could make it go however he wanted.

First, I had him take control of the rat in his fantasy and move it at will all around the living room, like one of those radio-controlled cars. Zip, zip, back and forth, wherever he wanted it to go, even across the ceiling. Then I had him play with its body. That is, I had him first shrink it way down to the size of a teeny-weeny dust speck, then bring it back up to regular rat-guy size. Then I had him puff it way up like a blimp till it filled the room, expanding into all the corners so it was stuck and couldn't move a whisker.

The whole time, I kept track of how he was feeling as he manipulated the pesky rodent, and a couple of times had him shrink the rat back down to a manageable size and start over. Finally, he settled on a form he liked. He made the rat very chubby, and about the size of a fat bunny. Then he turned the scary fangs into big buck teeth which hung over his lower lip as he sat up and begged. And gave him a checkered bow tie and a straw hat. For the final touch, he named the rat Rufous.

By the time he finished playing with his dream fantasy, he had tamed the Rat monster. He also went out to a toy store that week and bought himself a cute pink stuffed rat to keep in his living room. We never did get real psychological about it and interpret the symbolic meaning of the rat. There's always time to do that if Rufous shows up again...

CHAPTER 18

Dreams

Speaking of dreams, we might as well. Working with dreams is a kick. Since I prefer to be gentle and have fun with the client, I generally choose a Gestalt technique for dreamwork. I like this way of dealing with dreams partly because it's secretly rather psychological, and also because it doesn't preclude any of the other ways of looking at a particular dream. Freud, I expect, would be pleased.

First, I'll give away the secret psychological underpinnings of this method. The assumption is that even though we may fill our dreams with all manner of creatures and objects, anything in our dreams may be thought of as representing an aspect of ourselves -the dream is our creation, after all. So even if we make Mary, Queen of Scots, the protagonist in our dream, we can assume that she stands for some part of us.

It goes like this. In comes a client with an eerie dream she had last night and she wants to talk about it, because it's bothering her. Let's say she dreamed she was swimming in the ocean, really enjoying herself, when she noticed a barracuda lurking nearby. She turned toward shore, with the barracuda chasing her, and had almost made it to the beach when she woke up, feeling quite scared.

Usually, the client will already have done some interpretation on her own, like maybe the barracuda represents her upcoming exams or an older sister who used to harass her. And these interpretations are probably valid. If she wants to do some further exploring, however, I'll ask her to close her eyes and put herself back in the dream.

First, I'll have her be herself in the dream. I'll ask her to describe herself and what she's experiencing in some detail, while I write down or record what she says, asking occasional questions. Her account might go something like this. "I'm a young, single woman, not too bad looking. I'm nice to people. I work too hard, so I'm on vacation. I'm taking a swim. I have some friends, but I don't know where they are."

"That sort of bothers me, and it sort of bothers me too that I'm not at work. I'm not sure it's OK for me to be relaxing here and having a good time with all the work I have to do. I'm conscientious, and usually very reliable and dependable. But I'm pretty much enjoying myself until I see this shadow below me in the water. It's big, and as I look closer, I think it's a barracuda."

"I get real scared and start to swim for shore. I can see that the barracuda is following me - not too fast, but slowly closing in on me. I really want it to go away. I can see the beach. It's close, but I don't know if I'm going to make it, and just as I'm starting to really panic, I wake up."

Next, I'll have her stay in the dream, but this time, be the barracuda. "I'm long and scaly and dark and pretty old. I lie around in the shadows waiting to surprise something I can eat up, or at least scare. I like being big and powerful and scary. I see this girl above me and decide to go after her. I'm not really too hungry, but I like to chase her and scare her. I might take a bite out of her."

"I chase her. I can go real fast but I'm not trying too hard. I'm kind of lazy today and don't want to work too hard - I just want to have a little fun. I know I could catch up, but I don't want to work that hard. Anyway, I'm scaring her a lot."

When she's done with the fish, I'll have her be the ocean. "I'm huge and warm and kind of salty. I like the sun on me. I'm pretty calm today, not making any big waves. I have all kinds of stuff in me, most of which is way down deep out of sight. Some of what's in me is beautiful, like coral and bright fish. I also have lots of weeds and sunken debris at the bottom, and dangerous creatures in me."

"Some people are afraid of me because they aren't sure what's in me. This girl isn't afraid until she sees the barracuda that swims up out of me. She's surprised; she didn't know it was there. I watch her swim toward my shore. I'm not really too interested in whether she makes it or not."

Finally, I'll have her be the beach, the last element she mentioned in her dream. "I'm all white and beautiful. I sparkle. I'm crunchy and people walk on me and leave their footprints. I'm warm from the sun and very dry. I don't have any sharp rocks in me, so I'm easy to walk on. I'm not sure why I'm here, I just am. Maybe I need to be here so the ocean has edges; I contain it and keep it where it belongs."

"I don't need to know what my purpose is; I'm happy just being here. Lots of people like to visit me. I'm not paying much attention to what's going on out there in the water; it seems like some kind of contest. I'm not sure who's going to win. In the long run, it won't make a lot of difference to me. I don't think it has much to do with me. I'm just going to lie here and enjoy the sunshine."

Nifty, huh? At this point, I read or play back to her what she said as she was being each of the elements of her dream. This always elicits some wry and insightful grins as she considers whether the statements the "barracuda," the "ocean," and the "beach" made really do apply to her - whether she will own them as representing parts of herself. And if she acknowledges these aspects of herself, what does that mean to her? Especially, how does seeing herself in this broader way help her solve the original dilemma she brought into therapy?

Isn't therapy fun? Some of the unknowing self-descriptions people have given to themselves are marvelous. As a car - "I'm old and beat up. I sure don't look the way I used to, my paint's chipped and I have a few dents. I'm a little rusty and slow, but I still have a lot of good miles left in me..."

As a colt - "I'm young and very frisky. I love to gallop around creating mischief with the older horses. I hate being fenced in and am going to figure out a way to jump the fence one of these days and be free. I like to kick up my heels and chase butterflies. I switch my tail a lot when I'm frisky..."

As a house - "I'm big and old and empty. No one lives in me anymore, and I'm gradually falling into disrepair. My foundations are crumbling and I'm not too steady; I could probably fall down if a big enough wind came along. I used to have a happy family in me, though, and they loved me and took good care of me. Now I've been abandoned like an old relic. No one seems to care what happens to me now, and I'm very lonely. I wish someone new would move in and fix me back up."

As a river - "I'm very fast-moving and deep. I have enormous power. In some places I'm smooth and placid, but I can surprise people with my dangerous rapids. I have some huge rocks in me that have to be avoided or people can get hurt. People shouldn't try to navigate me unless they know what they're doing. In some places I'm dark and shadowed, and in other places the sun shines and I'm very bright. You can't see very far down into me, though, because I usually carry a lot of sediment and junk along with me..."

You're welcome to play with any of your dreams in this way. It's informative and fun. A caution, don't scare yourself if you've inserted something slimy or repulsive into one of your dreams. We all have primitive parts of ourselves that we think of in this way, so we can all bring up some slimy or repulsive feelings from time to time.

That's normal. Fortunately, most of these icky images stay safely tucked away in our unconscious part, where they belong. And remember, sometimes a barracuda is just a barracuda...

CHAPTER 19

Therapy School

I forget when I first started using this term. Quite awhile ago, for sure. I suppose, since I refer to it all the time in my work, and now I'm even writing a book about it, I ought to define it. So what the heck is Therapy School, anyhow? Defining T.S. is kinda complicated, since I mean different things by it at different times, in different contexts. And I reserve the right to continue to be inconsistent in this way. No, as a matter of fact, I don't care to work on it...

Now that I'm bringing the term under closer scrutiny, I can see that I have mainly two ways in which I use the term Therapy School. One is fairly traditional. This usage refers to the more or less formal education and training I went through, and continue to go through. These experiences produce, from time to time, pieces of paper which I can display on my walls as proof of my realness. You know, diplomas, certificates, that sort of thing. The best ones are printed in obscure, almost unreadable script, and feature shiny gold curlicues in the corners.

Interestingly, I notice that no two of mine have my name spelled exactly the same way. I think that's kind of cute. It keeps people on their toes - will the real therapist please stand up? And don't get me wrong, I'm extremely proud of all of these pieces of paper. I earned 'em, and it wasn't always easy! It's just that as the years roll on, I change my perspective on them and on what they mean.

First, some background. When I learned I'd been accepted to Stanford, I thought I'd died and gone to heaven. I still view the whole experience in a kind of little-kid-at-Christmas way, prompting my friends to react with tolerant amusement or even sometimes outright disgust. But to me it felt like the universe had opened up and invited me in to explore.

Possibility! Adventure! It seemed like a magical opportunity to move out of the world I was in and into some unknown, but definitely exciting, future. I know this sounds naive and childlike - it was. I'd certainly never in my 17 years expected to have a chance like that.

So off I went to Palo Alto, awestruck and picking the hay out of my teeth, so to speak. I spent the next four years being taught about psychology and sociology and anthropology and biology and religion and history and French. What I was learning in those four years was another story. Ultimately, I graduated with honors from what was one of the top psych departments in the country at the time. Did that mean anything about the kind of clinician I might be? Nope, not really.

Actually, I had started out in pre-med, since my script called for me to be a DOCTOR, but fortunately, I nearly flunked chemistry, so I got out of that. Phew! Just because I got out of pre-med, however, didn't mean that I was prepared to let go of my expectation (still largely out of my awareness) that I would spend my life in a Helping role. Psychology offered an avenue into helperdom that seemed interesting and only required amassing 45 units in my major. As I mentioned, I'm very curious about how things work, and about the nature of things, so I had the latitude to take a wide range of courses, and learn about a lot of stuff, while still staying within the parameters of my script. Clever, huh?

What did I learn? More to the point, what did I learn that has contributed to my effectiveness as a therapist? Here's what I think, about 25 years later. I think I learned a lot about myself and about life, which was more useful in my subsequent career as a psychotherapist (also in my careers as wife, mom, dog trainer, soccer player, etc.) than was learning a lot about Freud.

I'm sure this is no news to most of you reader folks. This is what young persons are supposed to be doing in those years of their lives, right? Well, I didn't know that, and felt rather guilty that I wasn't absorbing more psychology. And that I really liked my ethics and religion courses more than psychodynamics. And those existentialist guys! Wow, were they hard to read, but I knew there was some important stuff in there, if I could stick it out.

Anyhow, here are a few of the things I learned in undergraduate Therapy School. I found out that I could set pretty hard goals for myself and achieve them. Awkwardly, perhaps, but achieve them nevertheless. Finishing papers at three AM is much more dramatic than completing them days before they are due...

I also learned that getting good grades could have a lot more to do with following certain rules than with gaining new knowledge. And that a whole lot of what I grew up believing, well, it wasn't necessarily so. Uncomfortable learning, that one. Exchanging old familiar beliefs for new ones can be kind of disconcerting, even when the new ones are nicer.

For instance, I had packed my heavy duty self-badness filter in my trunk, along with my clothes and trinkets, and brought it with me to college. So I was prepared to continue to view myself as unattractive and not too nice to be near. But so many of these people seemed to like me. Huh? And I had dates. What was the deal here?

So, like the majority of persons my age, I was beginning to learn to grow up and be happy and satisfied in the world. A scholar, I wasn't.

I hadn't the foggiest idea how to be one. I did know how to get good grades, though, and there's something to be said for that.

What's the point in all this rhetoric? I guess it's that undergraduate Therapy School was helpful to me as a clinician, but not because of what I learned about Sigmund and those other psychological types. Rather, it was the beginning of my starting to change my early frame of reference, my ideas about myself, about others, and about life.

In a very real sense, Stanford was where I learned to dance. How many times did I Twist the Night Away...? I've lost count. It was also where I gave myself permission to dance, which is something else entirely. My kid part had grown up scared and rigid. I could have written the book on up-tight, but who would have wanted to read it?

And then I learned to dance. To rock. To swing. To twist. To polka. I even learned to do a mean limbo. A life that has dancing in it can't be all that dreadful, can it? If your therapist didn't love to dance, how could she possibly help you learn any fancy new steps?

Oh darn, now I've done it! I meant to sort of downplay the gee-whiz part of me in this book, and now I've gone and let it leak out all over. How am I going to look like a witty and urbane professional with all these stars in my eyes?

Oh well, that's part of who I are too, might as well admit it and get on with my story. OK, so what about the rest of Therapy School, formal variety? Was it as well-ordered and directed as my under-graduate experience? Yup. I got my Master's degree in Counseling because I couldn't figure out what else to do in Albuquerque.

You see, part of my learning at Stanford had included how to get married. And then how to move around with my husband's career. So here we were in, of all places, New Mexico. Quite a shock for a gal from the Great Green Pacific Northwest, let me tell you! I kept saying to my spouse, "I miss the beaches." His reply was cute, but not very satisfying. "You are on the beach," he would say, "you're just a long way from the water..."

So anyhow, I found the U. of N.M. and managed to convince them that I would stay there long enough to finish their two-year program. And I did, technically, even though the last part was completed by correspondence from Seattle. Meanwhile, I had produced Wally, and Beaver was in the oven.

So one of the things I learned in that part of Therapy School was that I could teach a statistics lab even though bulging. That was an interesting learning. It has helped me a lot as a therapist to know what it's like go through the challenges of being a young, inexperienced mom who thought she should sail through life, never minding how many hats she was trying to keep on her head at once.

It was in Seattle that I began to learn what it meant to be a clinician. With varying degrees of success, I had been trying my hand at being a kid-trainer, a dog-trainer, and a school psychologist. (We in the department always thought the term "School Psycho" was more fitting, so we used that most of the time)

I'd also been trying my hand at being a client. Perhaps I was prompted to do so in response to some of the activities mentioned above. It's hard to take when the dogs turn out to be smarter than you are... Fortunately, this is only true about 92% of the time. With kids, it's more like 98%, I'd say.

As a therapee, I was introduced to the Transactional Analysis branch of Therapy School. Intrigued, I decided to learn more about this model and began clinical TA training with Dr. Z. Looking back, I recognize that one of my unaware reasons for starting down this path was to fulfill my script directives by moving around to the other side of the couch. By finding folks to Help, so I could be Helpful.

So what else is new? I share this motivation with a great many of my colleagues. That doesn't mean we have to line up and burn our helper badges. It does suggest, however, that we shrink-types shouldn't avoid the client side of the couch, in case we need to sort out our unaware investments in being Helpful and separate them from our here-and-now, aware, reasons for choosing that role.

In fact, I learned a lot about being an effective therapist from being a successful (and unsuccessful) client. This is the less formal aspect of Therapy School. So, much of the time when I refer to T.S., I'm really talking about stuff I learned as a helpee. From that position, I know how crucial it is to me that my therapist genuinely cares about me and my welfare.

Nothing, absolutely nothing, has proven more healing to me than patient, loving, support when I was immersed in my self-badness. I have had the good fortune to find, and the smarts to stay with, therapists who knew how to connect with me from an I+ - Y+ position and were willing to take the risk of doing so. Were willing to become my partner for a few sets (or a few years) and teach me new ways of dancing.

Risk? Of course it's a risk. Any significant new relationship involves emotional risk for both partners. As soon as we let another become important to us, then we give that person the power to affect us deeply. Did you think it was only the client who had emotional reactions to how she was treated by the therapist? That it was only the client who cared what the therapist thought of her? No way.

So as a client, I learned from these folks what it's like to have a human being for a therapist. A human being who has clear enough ego boundaries to show me that he could be affected by me and yet that I in no way had to take care of him. That I couldn't take care of him, in fact, even if I tried. Slowly, in my guts, I learned the meaning of grown-up therapeutic altruism.

A new, individuated, dance. No Big Person needing a Little Person to take care of. These were Big folks, all right, Big enough and powerful enough to help me confront my script monsters, but they invited me to feel my Bigness and powerfulness, too. There's plenty of potency to go around.

They were also smart folks, very good at Meaning Attribution. Very good at explaining how humans worked, from the TA perspective as well as from the perspective of other branches of Therapy School. So the part of me that Wants Answers was satisfied.

And they showed me, by being comfortable with their playful and spunky kid parts, how to have fun at therapy, from either side of the couch. I confess that I was a rather slow and cautious learner here, having kept this part of me pretty much under wraps while surviving childhood, but, hey, who could resist this much fun? Who would want to?

I not only learned to poke fun at my script monsters, but also at the parts of me that were too serious, rather pompous, and Extremely Reasonable. Unfortunately, these parts seemed to have flourished during my time in traditional Therapy School, and so they required quite a bit of poking at to bring them down to manageable size. I don't worry about these parts getting out of hand now, though, because I know I can always count on my clients or my offspring to call them to my attention. And they know that they can always count on a gracious and appreciative reaction from me when they do...

Clients as teachers. Well, of course. Athletes are told that the best training for a sport is the playing of that sport. Same with therapists. Maybe that's why they call it being in practice. It's unavoidable, but the clients I work for now get better service from me than the ones I saw ten years ago, because they've been teaching me all along how to be a good shrink. This is one of the reasons I charged less dough back then.

It would be swell to be able to travel back through time and redo some of my work with clients. And I would love to have been in a more together place when I was raising my kids. Wouldn't we all? But it's absurd to think that any of us could have been other than as we were. Folks who spend much time fussing about the past in this way aren't living in this world and being satisfied with it. They are trying to live in the past and magically change it.

So it seems to me that the only sensible way to feel about what I have learned from clients over the years is appreciative. What have my client-professors taught me? Mainly, not to sell them short. Not to expect less than amazing courage and cleverness from them as they face down their particular monsters. That they are not fragile. (Have I made this point before? Oh, I have? Sorry...)

Well, belief in client resourcefulness and power is crucial. To underline it, I'll mention the client who was repeatedly sexually abused by his father. He endured it, but confronted his dad when it appeared that Dad was about to start in on Younger Brother. "I know where the guns and shells are kept," he told his father, "and if you ever touch either one of us again, I'll shoot you." The threat worked. This was one tough kid.

Clients also have taught me how to follow their lead. That I don't always have to be responsible for leading, for making sure they get what they came for. When I pay Good Enough attention, I notice that they'll take us in whatever direction we need to go, and that their tempo is just right. When my attention falters, we're likely to struggle over the lead until I come to my senses. Have a clue, Peg! How embarrassing.

Perhaps most importantly, they have given me permission to be a regular human being with them. It isn't always subtle, "Would you stop being a Therapist, Peg, and just be a regular person for a while?" Uh, well, OK, if you insist. I told you I don't get no respect...darned uppity clients. Raffleflax!

Or, "I didn't like what you just said to me, Peg. I think it was uncalled for and out of line." Sheese! Doesn't she know who I am? The nerve. After all, I was only trying to help. When I recover from my fit of righteous indignation, I take a look at what she's saying; she may have a point, which I'll have to grit my teeth and acknowledge. Yuck, I hate it.

Clients have even taught me that they can be nurturing toward me without our roles getting hopelessly tangled up and our boundaries going to pot. Right before group started one evening, I picked up my messages from my answering service. My husband had just left one telling me that my son was ill and had been admitted to the hospital.

The look on my face when I turned around from my desk must have said that something was very wrong. "What is it," asked one group member? I told them. "Do you have your car here?" "Yes." "Go." Just like that, "go." I went. They did group without me that night; what a lovely gift.

I'm not saying that what we all did there was right or wrong. It was neither. It was just another example of a simple, sensible, human interaction, which could have been seen as violating the boundaries of the therapeutic relationship. My view of this interaction, however, is that it was extremely therapeutic.

The phone message pointed out that I had a life outside the therapy room with real people in it who mattered to me, and who, for the moment, were interfering in my relationships with all of the clients present. Wouldn't it have been strange if I had not reacted strongly to that information about my son? My response was consistent with who they knew me to be through their own experiences.

Wouldn't it have been weird of me not to let them help me by sending me off? What on earth would I have been modeling then? Certainly not what I was trying to teach them about satisfaction in the real world (in which therapist's kids get sick), and happiness with self and others. I figured the only sensible thing to do was to thank them, which I did, then and later. At length.

Sensibleness. Now there's an interesting concept. Pat the Psychiatrist teaches unrelenting sensibleness. Always the foe of over-complication, he hammers away at Techniques that are Too Psychological. Sometimes he refers to his approach as "simple-minded" problem solving. We're not talking simplistic, here, just referring to peeling away the layers of complication that clients, and sometimes Therapy School, may have wrapped the problem in, resulting in its being hard to understand and solve.

It's taken me a lot of years and effort to learn to get this Simple. To Get that the effectiveness of an intervention is often inversely proportional to the number of syllables in it. In fact, clients sometimes complain a bit when they start to discover that their therapy is way simpler and easier than they expected. Maybe they're afraid they're not going to get their money's worth... Sometimes I offer to make things a little harder for a while if that will make them happier. Maybe I should get a sign to put over my door - "Character building stops here."

You may have guessed that some folks initially don't feel taken seriously enough if I fail to understand the extent of their self-badness. Or their felt necessity to examine every move for error or imperfection. They may even get a little miffed. They may especially get miffed if I don't agree with them about how bad others are or have been. Well, what I'm not taking seriously are their efforts to Gather Evidence in support of archaic script beliefs. After a while, they Get it.

Another reminder. Clients differ, and some of them need to take events in their lives more seriously, not less. The therapist, of course, needs to pay attention so she can tell the difference. By and large, though, doing therapy is much easier, less serious, and way more fun than they told me originally in Therapy School.

And more filling, too. Huh? Well see, there's this big controversy in T.S. about whether folks can do their therapy while eating or drinking. The prevailing wisdom seems to be that eating or drinking prevents, or at least seriously interferes with, therapeutic problem solving. Eating is out for sure, and coffee may be tolerable, but suggests a certain lack of attention to form.

I'm in a real fix, here. I keep admonishing my clients that they won't meet their therapeutic goals if they keep bringing in so much food, but they refuse to listen. What's a therapist to do? And, probably just to show me, they keep making their changes, seemingly oblivious to whether their mouths are full at the time. One group has developed a real culture around food rituals. I've started calling it the Food Group. Clients stand in line waiting for someone to graduate from that particular group so they can join it.

Some profs from Therapy School, formal variety, would say that the above group couldn't be called a psychotherapy group, then, but was rather a support group, or an encounter group, maybe. I suppose there is some truth to that, since what we do there is broader than psychotherapy. I insist, however, that one of the things we do in that group is very effective psychotherapy.

Few members have escaped from that group without having made remarkable life changes - internal changes that have made it possible for them to be more satisfied and happier with self and others. Changed their life scripts.

Actually, I don't really care what we call it - food group is fine. Because over its lifetime, the members have determined what it would turn into. I have served as a model, certainly, and have fulfilled the Executive Functions that keep it running fairly smoothly, but I never envisioned that it would evolve into the powerful healing force that it has. What a privilege have a part in creating an environment like that!

So I guess my main Therapy School professors now are my clients. I also draw liberally from any life experience that seems to have anything to do with satisfaction and happiness. I never miss reading the comics, for example. Great stuff there! Sci-fi and fantasy offer countless images and options as well. As do country western songs. And observations during my ferry commute. And soccer gatherings. For me, Therapy School is inescapable.

Want an example? Here's one. After soccer practice some years ago, a bunch of us were carrying on at a local tavern. I was sitting with two teammates, both good looking women. One of them kept being asked to dance by the local cowboys. The other, equally attractive, wasn't. Mystified, she asked the first woman her secret. In her wonderfully husky and sexy voice, my friend replied, "It's called Eye Contact, honey..."

Now, that's a natural for use in therapy. You'd be amazed at how much time we spend talking about issues involving Eye Contact. So this story comes in very handy. See how it works - life as Therapy School.

CHAPTER 20

Choosing a Therapist
(and a client)

My name and office phone number, of course, are listed in the telephone book. Somewhat to my surprise, I get a couple or three calls a month that way, from folks looking for a therapist. Maybe it's because my name starts with "B." Perhaps the "Q's" don't get that many. Come to think of it, I'm not sure there are any "Q's..."

At any rate, a person has to overcome a lot of Fear and Trembling to call a shrink, so I'm always surprised when they pull my name out of the hat, so to speak, without at least having gotten a recommendation from someone they know. A friend, a relative, a family doctor, the local service station attendant - somebody. I figure anyone who calls me cold must be very brave, indeed.

"Here's a name. Peg Blackstone, sounds like some kind of lawyer. Wonder if she's any good. Probably thinks she knows all the answers. I s'pose she charges an arm and a leg. Wonder if my insurance will cover it? Probably not, not counseling. I'll bet she'll think I'm really stupid to be upset over something like this. What would my friends think if they knew I was going to see a shrink? Sheese! Well, here goes..."

Sounds hard, doesn't it? You bet. I'm impressed that anyone does it. Most of my clients come to me because one of their friends gave them my name. Even so, the new person often waits a year or more before finally calling. Maybe they want to see whether their friend improves his life through his work with me, or whether he turns kind of far out and weird and psychological. Seems like a sensible precaution. Maybe they just have to reach a certain level of discomfort before taking the gamble. Not so sensible, perhaps, but understandable.

Some Therapy School professors suggest that it's best not to accept new folks who are referred by other clients, on the grounds that the referring agent becomes another party to the relationship. Triangulation might rear its ugly head, and the relationship would no longer involve the client and therapist only, but also the referring friend, as a sort of intruding ghost. I have found that to be true at times, but I just treat it as more grist.

Actually, it's probably rather rare that my relationship with a client never involves a third (or fourth, or eighth) party. Pat the Psychiatrist may become involved, or the client may bring their mom in with them a few times, or their infant, or perhaps their dog. Once we even had a bunny in group. And then there's group, of course, the ultimate in multiple relationships. So the therapeutic relationship in practice isn't so pristine. And it all still works.

Besides, I've never been able to figure out where these therapists who didn't accept client referrals got any business. I do get a fair number or referrals from docs and lawyers and other clinicians, but the bulk still come from other clients. I'd wonder about it if they didn't. Was it something I said? Something I didn't say? My deodorant...?

I tell neophyte therapists that they need only one client in order to be successful. Trouble is, this has to be a certain particular client, and she may not come along for a while. She must have three qualities. First, she must have a wide circle of friends or acquaintances. Second, she must think you, her therapist, are heaven's gift to clients. Third, she must be bossy. If she has all three, she (or he) will soon have you as busy as a little bee. She'll tell her friends you're the only therapist in the area who can help them, and they must go to you.

One client like this is really all any therapist needs, so if you're a shrink who has one and a second one happens to come your way, it might be nice not to take him on as a new client, but to send him along to some good theraperson you know who's just starting out in practice. It's only fair.

So that's how I get most of my folks. Now, what advice do I have to offer regarding how to choose a therapist for yourself? One point is obvious, ask some trusted friends who seem fairly squared away. Maybe you've had the chance to watch them make some changes of their own in therapy. Good.

However you get his name, the choosing is still up to you. Regardless of how well-recommended a therapist may have been, how much your friend swears by this guy, it's still your life, and your choice. I love to dance, but for some numbers only certain partners will do. Psychotherapy is a pretty important number. So I usually tell folks that the first meeting is for choosing. We each offer samples of ourselves to each other; here's my style, my approach, my manner, my dress, and so on. How do you like 'em?

This is a highly personal decision. Most of the stuff I've read about therapist-choosing seems to stress other factors, like background, fees, orientation, insurance reimbursement, experience, etc. Sort of like you could go to your neighborhood library and look up the Consumer Reports issue covering your local therapist models, and compare their ratings in these various categories, eventually deciding on the one with the highest overall standing. Or maybe second highest, if the highest didn't come in your favorite color.

A good way to choose a refrigerator or a VCR, but not a therapist, in my opinion. Not that all that stuff isn't important - it certainly is. And I'm quite relieved that our state has finally instituted a certification process for therapists, imperfect though any such system may be. Because until recently, Ragnar could have hung out his shingle advertising himself as, say, a marriage and family therapist, without any training or education in the field whatsoever.

Now the consumer can have some reassurance that the state, at least, thinks this person is qualified to do what they say they can. Folks who earn their living counseling others are also required to present each client with a disclosure statement which provides relevant data about the clinician's background, approach, and fees. Great. Knowing that information is necessary, but not sufficient.

Checking out qualifications is a grown-up function. Choosing a dance partner, though, like choosing a mate, or a puppy, or a favorite stuffed animal, is mostly done by the kid part of us. So, from among the therapists who look OK on paper, the client needs to chose one that seems (feels, looks, sounds, smells) right to the child part of him. And folks vary a lot in how much they credit their kid intuition.

Which presents an interesting dilemma. The more monsters a client has to tame, in other words, the worse trauma she's survived, the more important it is that she feels safe and yummy with her therapist. Who the therapist is as a human being, is much more significant than what she knows, or how she works. And yet, those same folks who had the roughest time as kids, may be the most split off from their intuitive parts.

So such a prospective client may talk herself out of paying attention to what her guts are telling her to do. This may work out all right, if she's picked a qualified clinician, because a trusting relationship can probably be built eventually. Things will get off to a better start, however, and proceed more swingingly, if the client feels comfortable and pretty safe right off the bat. Makes sense, doesn't it?

So I recommend face-to-face checking out. What's the waiting room like? Does it seem yummy to you? How does she greet you? Do you feel reassured or put off? How do you like her office? Does it invite you to put up your feet and relax? Does the therapist seem interested in whether you're comfortable? Is she paying attention? Do you like her? Do you like what she has to say?

The answers to these questions mostly won't be clearly thought out, they'll be more like impressions - thumbs up or thumbs down. Meet a few other shrinks and compare, if you want to. Ask any questions you have, including about fee arrangements, and see how you respond to her answers. You might think of it as rather like hiring a combination consultant and dance partner. She has to know what she's doing, and you have to hit it off too.

That's why I keep my Certificates of Realness prominently displayed, and also why I prominently display who I am in the first meeting. I have fun imagining what it's like for a client who's coming into my office for the first time. Right away, he checks out the various piles of paper I've filed on the floor. Some folks have even told me they breathed a sigh of relief when they saw the mess. (That's good, because it takes a lot of time each morning to get those piles strewn just right, artfully arranged in seeming randomness...)

Then he notices the bears of all sizes and colors in a heap by the couch. Then the framed poster featuring the cute rag doll who's just been through the wringer and shows it. And the drawer open with all the stickers hanging out of it every which way. And maybe the glittery tiara. And the coffee pot going.

Lots of overstuffed furniture and antiques and plants and comfortable mess. And out the windows the water and mountains. And dust on the window ledges, most likely. I'm imagining his kid part is intrigued, even though his grown-up parts may be disapproving or dubious. I'm probably not wearing sweats, since I've been so busy with the catalogs, but I'm certainly not Dressed for Success, either. My "look" depends on my mood and on what was ironed that morning, but it's always pretty relaxed. Good thing I have those diplomas and certificates up...

Is this person someone you'd trust your kid to? That makes it pretty easy, doesn't it? And that's what it boils down to for me, when I'm choosing a therapist. Does this person seem trustworthy and has he or she created a swell environment in which we can joke and play together, as well as work hard? Shall we dance...?

Then there's choosing a client. They don't say as much about this in Therapy School, so I thought I'd devote some time to the subject. As with choosing a shrink, some things are necessary, but not sufficient. Like I have to know how to work with the dilemmas this person presents. And I have to have some trust in their motivation to achieve their goals.

I had one new client from a nearby town who epitomized the attitude I look for. "How long do you think this process will take," she asked in the first meeting? Since she had brought in some impressive monsters to deal with, and was quite a long way from being happy with self and others, I suggested that she give herself a couple of years. "Well," she said, "I guess I'd better get a job here and move closer, so I can get on with it." Wowee! I had no doubts that she would achieve whatever she set out to do, therapeutically or otherwise.

If a client is willing to put that much of herself into the process, I have no reservations about matching her effort. I could hardly do less. I don't worry too much about whether we'll be able to do our therapeutic thing together, because I've found that I can dance with most anybody who wants to badly enough. I do look for one other quality besides sincerity and motivation, however, and that's a sense of humor. Or at least a possible sense of humor. A glimmer, down in there somewhere.

I don't care much what his Therapy School diagnosis, if any, might be. That's why nature made referral sources, I figure, to be there if we need 'em. But humor as a therapeutic option is central to the way I work, so the client who hangs around very long with me has to be willing to accept that quirk, annoying as he may find that at first. I see humor as darned near essential to satisfaction, and happiness with self and others. How could anyone risk the awkwardness of trying new dance steps unless they could laugh at themselves and the whole situation?

CHAPTER 21

Props

My clients accept a lot of other weird stuff from me too, besides humor and nosiness. Like the props. You know, those articles laying around the room that I mentioned earlier? The bears, for instance. I'm really not into bears, you understand, they just seemed to multiply. I guess it's my fault, I started it. I found this great bear in California that was just three-year-old size, and before we knew it, Ragnar and I were taking him home, strapped carefully into his own seat on the plane.

My office is fairly big, since I do groups in it - and, well, he looked kind of lonely. So pretty soon I found a smaller, cushier companion bear-guy. And then one of my clients discovered a panda on one of her business trips that showed up in her suitcase when she was unpacking. Imagine her surprise! And then a co-leader left and presented us with a medium sized brown bear-gal. And so on...

Anyhow, we now have almost enough bears to go around during group. Now and then one of them goes home with someone for a spell, or takes a trip in a suitcase, or some such. And they've all absorbed more tears and slobber than you could imagine. They're quite patient about it, and about being tightly squooshed and squozen now and again, in the midst of someone's work. If I'm in the mood, I may even hold one while I'm listening to a client, but I hardly ever slobber.

I don't want to leave out my new pink pig. She's battery powered and grunts fetchingly when turned on. (So do some people I know...) Anyhow, this charming pig also walks and wiggles her tail. Some dear friends gave her to me as a birthday present last year after only a minor amount of begging on my part. Everyone agrees that the Rhinestone earrings I put on her piggy ears add a nice touch. It's really hard for any of us to take ourselves too seriously with her around.

Then there are the stickers. They multiplied too. See, they started out as a few stars - you know, the kind teachers used to put on our papers at school - the kid part of most everybody gets a kick out of that familiar kind of recognition. The stuffy part of a client may turn down a snazzy sticker for some great work, but the kid part of them is turned on. In my overflowing drawer, I've got all kinds of fantastic stickers - stars, rainbows, animals, hearts, vehicles, candies, and even light bulbs for folks who have big insights.

Clients don't have to do anything to earn them, either, some just come in and grab a couple to start out with. Or they give me one if they think I was especially therapeutic that day. Sometimes in group a member will take charge of the drawer, pull it out, and start handing out the stickers they think are just right for their fellow groupees. Sticker response really points out how someone is feeling about themselves too. "Oh no, I don't want a sticker for that. It was nothing." "Oh OK, well then how about tearing off just a corner of one if that's all you deserve? Maybe next week you might do some work that's worth a whole one..."

I've ordered a real light bulb that lights up when you hold it in your hand, but it hasn't arrived yet. I can hardly wait. And I have a little buzzer which produces six different sounds, each more obnoxious than the last, to use in response to particularly blatant self-discounts. The tiara is for birthdays and other special occasions, or for any time anyone feels like wearing a crown. Birthdays also rate balloon and candle stickers, and maybe treats, if someone brought them.

There have been numerous threats about whoopie cushions, especially when someone new is joining group, but so far, we've been spared. Since I've already done my time with teen-aged males, I appreciate that. Often clients will set up their own "props show-and-tell" when they've been given some outrageous and unreasonable homework calling for the purchase of Silly String or a squirt gun, or some such. They always seem to want to bring the new toy in to demonstrate.

My favoritest squirt gun is one that looks like hollow space-cadet goggles with the squirt hole between the eyes. Have you seen it? There's a long tube leading from behind the ear down the arm and ending with a large bulb. When you squeeze the bulb, you nail whoever you're looking at. After a certain amount of experimentation, I've found that an absolute dead-pan expression while squirting has the most dramatic flair. No home should be without one; ours certainly isn't.

But then, I just might have the most extensive squirt gun collection this side of Washtucna. If you're looking for all-around versatility, I recommend one of the battery-powered types. If Kitty ventures onto the dining room table, I can wing her from across the living room with one of those hummers. They have big reservoirs too, so they're great for summer water fights with Wally and Beaver.

Cartoons make good props too. You can have them in a scrap book in your waiting room, if you like. This method of display would offer new clients an intriguing chance to begin to wonder what they were in for in hiring you. I prefer to put them up on my office bulletin board. That way, if things should get a little slow, the client or I can get up and do a bit of light reading. Have you noticed the proliferation of good shrink cartoons? Wonderful material.

Since I totally missed the class on Props in Therapy School, I've had to improvise. My selection is highly individualized, so don't take it as a standard, just as a permission. Bob Goulding has a cow bell, and Pat the Psychiatrist has a rubber chicken, so you can see that it's a matter of taste. I also have a foam brick, but I stole it from Beaver, so don't let on. He deserved it anyway, because he always pooks the nose of my favorite bear in when he visits my office.

CHAPTER 22

Stuff I Hate to Admit

Maybe I should leave out this section...nah, might as well fess up. More good modeling, right? Well, let's see, one thing I hate to admit is how bent out of shape I can sometimes get when folks won't let me Help them with my well-intentioned and well-thought-out advice. After all, I have been to Therapy School, you know.

I guess I shouldn't feel too bad about my opinions being ignored, though, because I'm in good company. One evening in my former life I was watching a talk show. The guest was John Kenneth Galbraith, a most imposing and impressive gentleman. A diplomat and statesman. He was telling of his adventures with Uncle Sam while serving as ambassador to India, I believe.

It seems that Mr. Galbraith had gone to a great deal of trouble to research a certain sensitive local topic and had sent the information off to DC. Evidently, he was expecting an immediate reply, and when he received none, he inquired as to why. The response? "Your opinions, insofar as they have any merit, have already been considered and rejected."

What? Someone actually said this to John Kenneth Galbraith? It's hard for me to imagine anyone having the temerity to make such a statement to this man. I mean, really. So I suppose if they can do that to someone of his stature, I shouldn't be too shocked when a client sends me the same message. Maybe I'll learn to handle such responses the same way he did, with amusement, rather than indignation.

Let's see, what else do I hate to admit? Well, sometimes I'm less than gracious about 'fessing up to mistakes. Way less. I've even been known, when confronted with an error I couldn't weasel out of, to pound my fists on my chair, stamp my feet and declare through clenched teeth, "I hate it, I hate it..."

And I really hate to admit that I'm sometimes pompous. Yech, how embarrassing. Fortunately, I can laugh at myself. Eventually. Now that I look over these things I hate to own up to, I see that they all come from the parental part of me. Hmmm. My teenaged children, of course, were invariably understanding and kind when they pointed such attributes out to me. Thanks, guys.

Then there's this one incident I sort of hate to admit and I sort of don't, all at the same time. One time there was a difficult member in group and I just wasn't dealing effectively with this person. Clearly, it was another instance of someone being much better at staying stuck than I was at being Helpful, but I guess I was too stubborn to admit defeat yet.

As usual in situations like this, the group process was hung up until this struggle could be resolved. People were all getting pretty frustrated, because they wanted this person to either start using the group to problem solve (become a working member of the group team) or leave. And I wasn't making that happen. It's sort of like in a family; if a parental unit appears unable to take care of business, the kids will step in. That's what they did. Eventually, the group members took over and solved the problem pretty much on their own while I sort of sat back and watched.

What was weird (and wondrous) about the situation was that while the group members were functioning more effectively at solving the group problem than I was, I knew that they had learned most of the skills to solve it through their work with me. They never warned me about that in Therapy School, either. See why I love this work?

Which brings me to the last thing I don't want to admit. I feel sort of like I'm cheating. Huh? Well see, I get to run my own business. Within professional, ethical and legal guidelines, I get to do it however I want. I can set my own hours, choose my own clients, decorate my office the way I want, work at the seashore, dress the way I want to, and do very little paperwork. To top it all off, I get paid for giving my opinions and sometimes my advice. What a deal!

Further, I get to work with the swellest people in the world, be successful, and have a great time. I even get to write books. Somehow, I never learned in T.S. that shrinking could be this much fun. It's so neat that sometimes my kid part still magically fears that "they" might find out and not let me do it any more. I know that sounds pretty weird, but just in case, please don't tell a soul how great I've got it, OK?

CHAPTER 23

Things My Mother Told Me

It's funny, the older I get, the more I value old things. Sometimes even the things I hated as a kid, like anchovies. Maybe someday Wally and Beaver will even value those family meetings - right after hell freezes over...

Well anyway, I think back from time to time over some of the old family wisdom I grew up with - some of the stuff that has influenced me without my realizing it. Like the little painted plate that hung on the wall behind the stove in our one-fanny kitchen. (One-fanny kitchen, you know, one that's so narrow that two people can't pass each other in it.) Anyhow, my mom had carefully lettered these words of wisdom on this little plate, "Man works from sun to sun, but women's work is never done." Hmmm.

How many of us grew up with that? Lots. And most of us never suspected the influence of that sort of belief, even though we could look around us at a nation of super-women, managing to keep any number of balls in the air at once, and more importantly, thinking nothing of it. Interesting, isn't it? I remember looking at that little plate and thinking it was pretty, and sort of wondering why someone would make up a saying like that. I never asked my mother why she put it up there; maybe sometime I will.

I didn't feel victimized by that attitude, or resentful of men. They, of course, are influenced by their own cultural and family directives, but I'm just musing about some of the attitudes I responded to in growing up. More informal Therapy School. I think I took that particular saying mostly as a permission to achieve.

Especially since I had another, verbal directive from my mom, which I've learned was a rather unusual one for a mother to give her daughter at the time. It was this: "Being female is swell, and certainly doesn't limit what you can do in the world." I grew up thinking everybody believed that, but I have occasionally run into some more restrictive attitudes. I mostly ignore them, what do they know?

She didn't stop there, on top of all this, she also told me that I would enjoy life more the older I got. Wow! What a great permission. As you may have noticed, I have taken it and run with it. Literally. At 48, I'm one of the younger women on my current geriatric soccer team. Our joints are failing and gravity is taking its toll, but we're still going strong. We're just going strong more slowly these days.

The main difference I notice, however, is off the field. When we started playing, most of us in our early thirties, our after soccer get-togethers featured talk and naughty jokes about the men or potential men in our lives. Now it tends to feature cosmetic surgery. A little nip here, a little tuck there, and things will look just about the way they used to, right? Well, practically.

We'll never give up on the naughty jokes, though. And some of us have bought the sweatshirts that say, "Old age and treachery will overcome youth and skill." We're all kind of uppity - I love it. Our partners have to learn to be pretty tolerant. One of my friends has a different sort of sign over her stove. Hers says, "We interrupt this marriage to bring you the soccer season."

Some of our spouses shake their heads at our insistence on playing till we drop. One teammate's husband tells all their friends that he's expecting her to quit soon, since "she has about 15 minutes left in her knees." Ragnar, a geriatric athlete himself, greets all this with an attitude of amused tolerance. I suspect that somewhere down in his little Norswedish soul he's rather proud of me. (It's sometimes hard to tell with Scandinavians, you know.) He did point out to me a new popular Japanese-American word, "obattalion," which means "a pushy middle-aged woman." I'm not quite sure why he felt the need to call this word to my attention, but I rather like it, don't you? Help yourself.

Speaking of terms, the women in my family passed on some colorful expressions. Like "You"d better not do that, or I'll jump down your throat and teeter on your wishbone." I never could figure out how that would work, but it gave me pause. Another one was "Don't get your tail in a knot." Cute, huh?

One of my grandmother's that I like to use with clients is dif-fic-ulties. (emphasis on the "fic") "That's quite a dif-fic-ulty, all right." Or, "The dif-fic-ulty with that is...") See how it normalizes and makes problems seem manageable? Turn something into a dif-fic-ulty instead of a major trauma or character flaw and you can have fun dealing with it. Less fear and trembling.

Don't you hate it when something annoying your mother told you over and over turns out to be true? I'm still waiting for this sort of concession from my sons. Anyhow, my mom was always telling me to sit up straight, and I've recently had to admit she was right. My doctor had a scientific explanation for it. "There's gooshy stuff in your backbone," she said, "and if you don't sit up straight and preserve your lordosis, the gooshy stuff pooches out and pinches your nerves."

She even gave me an informative little pamphlet extolling the virtues of lordosis. (Lordosis is the curve in one's lower back that evidently must be preserved, if you value your gooshy stuff.) After receiving this scientific explanation and reading my lordosis pamphlet, I had to admit that Mom had been right again, and I would get pains in my leg if I disobeyed.

I must have been following mother's directive pretty well all along, however, because of a comment my friend Karen (of belching and farting fame) made about me. "Peg's a lot like me when she does therapy," she told a client she was referring to me, "except that she sits up straighter." I wasn't quite sure how to take that one. You wait and see, though, I'll bet when we're both old and grey she's going to really envy my swell lordosis...

As I've mentioned, therapersons such as myself were often directed as kids to be Helpful. How? Here's an illustrative little vignette. One sunny day in the summer of my eighth year, my family was enjoying an outing at a local lake. A bunch of us kids were playing out on the end of the dock when one of the younger tots fell into the water near the shore. The rest of us watched in frozen startlement as a parent rushed in and pulled the scamp out.

All was fine. What I remember about the scene, though, is hearing mom say to a friend, "I can't understand why Peggy didn't jump in and pull her out." Hmmm. I got the picture. Probably had nothing whatsoever to do with my becoming a life guard in high school...

This parent-kid scene can seem really tricky, can't it? Somehow, we mostly get through its ups and downs and end up pretty good friends. And there are occasional shining moments, when your child actually acknowledges you in some way. I'm thinking of one particular concession I got from a son.

You see, when Beaver was fifteen, he ignored my caution about the condition of the brakes on his bike, and had a close encounter with the pavement, which resulted in his breaking his crown. Years later, in a fit of generosity, he managed to squeeze out an admission from between clenched teeth that maybe he should have listened to me about the brakes. We mothers have to hold on to these gems - they can be few and far between.

Bibliography and Recommended Reading

Bibliography
Real Therapy School Books

1. American Psychiatric Association: *Diagnostic and Statistical Manual of Mental Disorders*, Third Edition, Washington, D.C., A.P.A. (1980) (The Big Green Book.)

2. Bass, E. & Thornton, L., Eds, (1983) *I Never Told Anyone*. New York: Harper and Row. (Writings by women who were sexually abused as children.)

3. Berne, E. (1972) *What do you say after you say Hello?* New York: Grove Press. (Berne developed Transactional Analysis.)

4. Berne, E. (1966) *Principles of Group Treatment*. New York: Oxford University Press.

5. Berne, E. (1964) *Games People Play*. New York: Grove Press.

6. Berne, E. (1961) *TA In Psychotherapy*. New York: Grove Press.

7. Blackstone, P. (1987) *Loving Too Much - Disease or Decision?* Transactional Analysis Journal, 17, (4), 185-190. (Critique of the book *Women Who Love Too Much*, by Robin Norwood.)

8. Butler, S. (1978) *Conspiracy of Silence*. San Francisco: Volcano Press. (A good book about incest.)

9. Cousins, N. (1989) *Head First - the biology of hope*. New York; Penguin Books. (Good reading on mind-body interaction.)

10. Eisler, R. (1987) *The Chalice and the Blade*. San Francisco: Harper and Row. (An anthropologist's look at "her story," very intriguing.)

11. Goulding, M.M. & Goulding, R. (1979) *Changing Lives through Redecision Therapy*. New York: Bruner/Mazel. (All of their books are great for therapists and for clients.)

12. Goulding, M.M. & Goulding, R. (1980) *The Power is in the Patient.* San Francisco: Transactional Publications. (See above.)

13. Goulding, M.M. & Goulding, R. (1989) *Not to Worry.* New York: William Morrow. (Good homework for folks who tend to fuss.)

14. Haley, J. (1973) *Uncommon Therapy.* New York: W.W. Norton & Company. (I like what he's written about Milton Erickson.)

15. Halpern, H. (1976) *Cutting Loose.* New York: Simon & Schuster. (One of the better self-help books, I recommend it to all my new clients.)

16. Halpern, H. (1982) *How to Break Your Addiction to a Person.* New York: McGraw-Hill. (I like it, even though I don't agree with his use of the term "addiction.")

17. James, M. & Jongeward, D. (1971) *Born to Win.* Menlo Park: Addison-Wesley. (A classic, very useful, as are all of Muriel James's books.)

18. Johnson, S. (1985) *Characterological Transformation - The Hard Work Miracle.* New York; Norton. (A "must read," along with his other book, for therapists; extremely humane.)

19. Johnson, S. (1987) *Humanizing the Narcissistic Style.* New York; Norton. (Lovely.)

20. Kadis, L., Ed. (1985) *Redecision Therapy - Expanded Perspectives.* Watsonville: Western Institute for Group ad Family Therapy. (Varied examples of using redecision therapy.)

21. Kaufman, G. (1985) Shame: *The Power of Caring.* Rochester, VT; Schenkman Books. (A lovely, healing book about a type of narcissistic injury - great for therapists and clients both.)

22. Lieberman, M.A., Yalom, I., & Miles, M. (1973) *Encounter Groups; First Facts.* New York; Basic Books. (Study showing effective leadership qualities.)

23. Shinoda-Bolen, J. (1985) *The Goddesses in Every Woman.* New York; Harper & Row. (An affirming Jungian book about women and mythology.)

24. Spitz, R. (1945) *Hospitalism, Genesis of Psychiatric Conditions in Early Childhood.* Psychoanalytic Study of the Child 1; 53-74. (Shows the biological importance of strokes.)

25. Stanford Observer, (Jan/Feb 1990) School of Education Insert. Stanford; Stanford News Service.

26. Steiner, C. (1974) *Scripts People Live.* San Francisco; Grove Press. (Lots of good stuff about TA, and especially about strokes.)

27. Stewart, I., & Joines, V., (1987) *TA Today*. Chapel Hill; Life Space Publishing. (Finally, a complete TA primer - very well done.)

28. Tavris, C. (1990) *The Politics of Codependency*. The Family Therapy Networker, Jan/Feb, 43.

29. Torrey, F. (1985) *Surviving Schizophrenia*. New York; Harper & Row. (Very useful for anyone with a mentally ill family member.)

30. Treadway, D. (1990) *Codependency: Disease, Metaphor, or Fad?* The Family Therapy Networker; Jan/Feb, 39-42.

31. Yalom, I. (1974) *Every Day Gets a Little Closer: A Twice-told Therapy*. New York; Basic Books. (Co-authored with Ginny Elkin, a personal therapy account from both sides of the couch.)

32. Yalom, I. (1975) *The Theory and Practice of Group Psychotherapy*. New York; Basic Books. (A classic - I use it in my Group Treatment Training, along with Berne and Gouldings.)

33. Yalom, I. (1980) *Existential Psychotherapy*. New York; Basic Books. (Helpful and easy to read consideration of existential issues which we all face.)

34. Yalom, I. (1989) *Love's Executioner and other tales of psychotherapy*. New York; Basic Books. (Case histories, very interesting.)

Recommended Reading

Fun, Fantasy, and other Fiction.
(Homework for you, if you like.)

(These are authors I read for relaxation and entertainment, and whom I recommend frequently to clients for homework.)

Patrick McManus - great corny humor, teaches how to be a kid - *A Fine and Pleasant Misery; They Shoot Canoes, Don't They?; Never Sniff a Gift Fish; The Grasshopper Trap; Rubber Legs and White Tail Hairs; The Night the Bear Ate Goombah.*

C J Cherryh - all, especially the "Chanur" series, wonderful powerful heroines, swashing and buckling around space - *Pride of Chanur; Chanur's Venture; The Kif Strike Back; Chanur's Homecoming.*

Frank Herbert - all, especially the "Dune" series, very psychological, terrific women!

Marion Zimmer Bradley - all, especially her "Darkover" series and *The Mists of Avalon*.

Anne McCaffrey - all, her "Dragonriders of Pern" series is marvelous.

Jennifer Roberson - all, full of uppity women and adventure.

David Eddings - all, especially the "Belgariad" and "Mallorean" series - characters interrelate with high humor, lots of love, and no excuses.

Roger Zelazny - all, especially his "Amber" series - very magical, hero laughs at himself engagingly.

Elizabeth Moon - all, you guessed it, more uppity women.

Betty MacDonald - all - I liked *The Plague and I* the best, written in the 40's.

Peg Bracken - preceded Erma Bombeck, but of same genre, *I Hate to Cook Book; I Hate to Housekeep Book*.

John L. Anderson - *Scandinavian Humor and Other Myths* - good companion to Garrison Keillor.

Garrison Keillor - all, start with *Lake Wobegon Days*.

Lisa Alther - *Other Women* - a fictional (?) therapy journey.

Sheila Ballantyne - *Imaginary Crimes* - lovely story of an isolated child with very dysfunctional parents.